SEQUELS

compiled by

Dorne Fraser

Volume 2
Junior Books

LONDON
ASSOCIATION OF ASSISTANT LIBRARIANS
(GROUP OF THE LIBRARY ASSOCIATION)
Published with assistance from
HOLMES McDOUGALL BOOKSELLING, NEWCASTLE UPON TYNE
1984

ISBN 0 900092 47 5

Previous editions included in *Sequels*:

1922, by Thomas Aldred

1928, by W. H. Parker

1947, by F. M. Gardner

1955, by F. M. Gardner

1967, by F. M. Gardner

Sequels Vol. 2: Junior Books, 1976 (reprinted 1978),
compiled by F. M. Gardner and Lisa-Christina Persson

Printed in Scotland by Macdonald Printers (Edinburgh) Limited

PREFACE TO THE SEVENTH EDITION

This edition of *Junior Sequels* is the second to be published in a separate volume to *Adult Sequels*. The two, however, remain as companion volumes and many titles previously listed in both works have now been removed from this volume. Works intended for 'young adults', such as books by Paul Zindel and Gunnel Beckman, are retained in *Junior Sequels*. The factors governing inclusion remain the same as in previous editions:

a) stories featuring the same character or group of characters;

b) stories with a connected narrative or theme;

c) stories connected by historical or geographical means.

In this edition a considerable effort has been made to date, where possible, all the titles included. In the case of American and European works the dates given are for first publication in the United Kingdom. Many authors and titles present in previous editions have been omitted from this volume as it was felt that they were no longer of current interest or not easily available. Among the works included for the first time are the 'Peanuts' books of Charles Schulz and Roger Hargreaves' 'Mr Men' and 'Little Miss' books; these are taken from *British Books in Print* and are listed strictly in date order. Other authors continuing well-established and well-loved series are Mary Norton (*The Borrowers Avenged*) and P. L. Travers (*Mary Poppins in Cherry Tree Lane*).

A new feature is the separate listing of award winners at the back of the volume, which includes among others Carnegie, Kate Greenaway, Newbery and Caldecott medal winners. New sequels are constantly appearing so that no list can ever be complete, any suggestions for inclusion in future editions of *Junior Sequels* would be welcome.

Inevitably, this edition of *Junior Sequels* reached completion due to the efforts of a number of people. Ruth Kaye of Askews kindly sent notices of new publications; Andrew Bethune, Margaret Corr, Gill Daley and Evelyn Smith studied the manuscript and offered valuable suggestions and Irene Miller re-typed the manuscript. As always the final responsibility for any errors remains with the author.

Dorne Fraser.

Adams, Agnes

1 Doddles: a school story 1920
2 Doddles makes things hum 1927

Adamson, Gareth

1 Mr Budge builds a house 1963
2 Mr Budge buys a car 1965

Adamson, Jean *and* Gareth

1 Topsy and Tim's Monday book 1960
2 Topsy and Tim's Tuesday book 1960
3 Topsy and Tim's Wednesday book 1961
4 Topsy and Tim's Thursday book 1961
5 Topsy and Tim's Friday book 1962
6 Topsy and Tim's Saturday book 1962
7 Topsy and Tim's Sunday book 1962
8 Topsy and Tim's foggy day 1962
9 Topsy and Tim at the football match 1963
10 Topsy and Tim go fishing 1963
11 Topsy and Tim's bonfire night 1964
12 Topsy and Tim's snowy day 1964
13 Topsy and Tim go on holiday 1965
14 Topsy and Tim at the seaside 1965
15 Topsy and Tim on the farm 1970
16 Topsy and Tim's paddling pool 1970
17 Topsy and Tim at school 1971
18 Topsy and Tim at the zoo 1971
19 Topsy and Tim go to hospital 1971
20 Topsy and Tim's birthday party 1971
21 Topsy and Tim go pony-trekking 1972
22 Topsy and Tim go safely 1972
23 Topsy and Tim take no risks 1973
24 Topsy and Tim learn to swim 1973
25 Topsy and Tim go hill-walking 1973
26 Topsy and Tim go sailing 1974
27 Topsy and Tim cross the channel 1974
28 Topsy and Tim in Belgium 1974
29 Topsy and Tim in Holland 1974
30 Topsy and Tim visit the dentist 1975
31 Topsy and Tim's new brother 1975
32 Topsy and Tim visit the doctor 1975
33 Topsy and Tim at the wedding 1976
34 Topsy and Tim's new school 1976
35 Topsy and Tim's pet show 1976
36 Topsy and Tim visit the Tower of London 1976
37 Topsy and Tim go camping 1977
38 Topsy and Tim go shopping 1977
39 Topsy and Tim at the circus 1977
40 Topsy and Tim's sports day 1977
41 Topsy and Tim at the fair ground 1978
42 Topsy and Tim at the library 1978
43 Topsy and Tim at the vet's 1978
44 Topsy and Tim choose a puppy 1978
45 Topsy and Tim meet the monsters 1978
46 Topsy and Tim's picnic 1978
47 Topsy and Tim's school outing 1978
48 Topsy and Tim's train journey 1978
49 Topsy and Tim move house 1979
50 Topsy and Tim at the hairdresser 1979
51 Topsy and Tim go in an aeroplane 1979
52 Topsy and Tim have a barbecue 1979
53 Topsy and Tim at the fire-station 1979
54 Topsy and Tim at the jumble sale 1979
55 Topsy and Tim at the pantomime 1979
56 Topsy and Tim's caravan holiday 1979
57 Topsy and Tim's ABC 1982
58 Topsy and Tim's counting book 1982
59 Topsy and Tim have their eyes tested 1982
60 Topsy and Tim help the dustmen 1982
61 Topsy and Tim's new playground 1982
62 Topsy and Tim's school play 1982

'Adventures of Topsy and Tim' 1970, 'Hallo Topsy and Tim' 1971, 'Surprises for Topsy and Tim' 1971, 'Topsy and Tim out and about' 1973, 'Topsy and Tim in Europe' 1974 are omnibus volumes containing two or more in the series. From No. 33 the series is in a smaller format, 'Handy Books' and several of the earlier books have been republished in the new format.

TOPSY AND TIM ACTIVITY BOOKS:

1 Topsy and Tim can print in colour 1980
2 Topsy and Tim can garden 1980
3 Topsy and Tim can look after their pets 1981
4 Topsy and Tim can play party games 1981
5 Topsy and Tim can cook 1981
6 Topsy and Tim can sing and play 1981
7 Topsy and Tim can make music 1982
8 Topsy and Tim help birds 1982

Ahlberg, Allan *and* Janet

THE BRICK STREET BOYS:

1 Here are the Brick Street Boys 1975
2 A place to play 1975
3 Sam the referee 1975
4 Fred's dream 1976
5 The great marathon football match 1976

TWO HEADS:

1 The one and only Two Heads 1979
2 Two wheels Two Heads 1979

Aiken, Joan

THE ARMITAGE FAMILY:

1 All you've ever wanted and other stories 1953
2 More than you bargained for and other stories 1955
Also available in one volume, 'All and more' 1971.

MORTIMER THE RAVEN:

1 Arabel's raven 1972
2 The escaped black mamba 1973
3 The bread bin 1974
4 Mortimer's tie 1976
5 Mortimer and the sword excalibar 1979
6 Arabel and Mortimer 1980
7 Mortimer's portrait on glass 1981
8 Mortimer's cross 1983
'Tales of Arabel's raven' 1973 is an omnibus edition of Nos 1-3. 6 contains 4 and 5 and a new story 'The spiral staircase'.

JAMES III ENGLAND SERIES:

1 The wolves of Willoughby Chase 1962
2 Black hearts in Battersea 1965
3 Night birds on Nantucket 1966
4 The stolen lake 1981
5 The cuckoo tree 1971
□
1 Go saddle the sea 1977
2 Bridle the wind 1983

Ainsworth, Ruth

RUFTY TUFTY SERIES:

1 Rufty Tufty the golliwog 1952
2 Rufty Tufty at the seaside 1954
3 Rufty Tufty goes camping 1957
4 Rufty Tufty runs away 1958
5 Rufty Tufty flies high 1959
6 Rufty Tufty's island 1960
7 Rufty Tufty and Hattie 1962
8 Rufty Tufty makes a house 1965

CHARLES SERIES:

1 Charles stories and others, from "Listen with Mother" 1954
2 More about Charles and other stories, from "Listen with Mother" 1954
3 Five "Listen with Mother" tales about Charles 1957

SHELLOVER SERIES:

1 The ten tales of Shellover 1963
2 Tales of Shellover 1967
3 More tales of Shellover 1968

Akrill, Caroline

1 Eventer's dream 1981
2 A hoof in the door 1982

Alcott, Louisa May

AUNT JO'S SCRAP-BAG SERIES:

1 My boys 1872
2 Shawl-straps 1874
3 Cupid and Chow-Chow 1874
4 My girls 1878
5 Jimmy's cruise in the *Pinafore* 1879
6 An old-fashioned Thanksgiving 1882

THE COUSINS:

1 Eight cousins 1874
2 Rose in bloom 1876

LITTLE MEN AND LITTLE WOMEN SERIES:

Published under varying titles but originally as:
1 Little women 1868
2 Good wives 1869
3 Little men 1871
4 Jo's boys 1886

Aldridge, Alan

1 The butterfly ball and the grasshopper's feast 1973
2 Peacock party 1979

Alexander, Lloyd

CHRONICLES OF THE KINGDOM OF PRYDAIN:

1 The book of Three 1966
2 The black cauldron 1967
3 The castle of Llyr 1968
4 Taran wanderer 1967
5 The High King 1968

Allan, Mabel Esther

1 The Ballet family 1963
2 The Ballet family again 1964
□
1 A school in danger 1952
2 Over the sea to school 1950
3 At school in Skye 1957

WOOD STREET SERIES:

1 The Wood Street group 1970
2 The Wood Street secret 1968
3 The Wood Street rivals 1971
4 The Wood Street helpers 1973

5 Away from Wood Street 1976
6 Wood Street and Mary Ellen 1979
7 Strangers in Wood Street 1980
8 Growing up in Wood Street 1982
Stories about a group of children in Liverpool.

PINE STREET SERIES:
1 Pine Street pageant 1978
2 Pine Street goes camping 1980
3 Pine Street problem 1981
4 Goodbye to Pine Street 1982
5 Alone at Pine Street 1983

Allen, Eric
1 Pepe Moreno 1957
2 Pepe Moreno and the roller skates 1958
3 Pepe on the run 1959
4 Pepe Moreno and the dilapidated donkey 1960
5 Pepe Moreno's quixotic adventure 1962

Allen, Joy
1 Teeth for Charlie 1976
2 Boots for Charlie 1978
3 Stitches for Charlie 1980
4 Cup final for Charlie 1981

Allen, Merritt Parmelee
1 The mudhen 1946
2 The mudhen and the walrus 1950
3 The mudhen acts naturally 1955

Almqvist, B.
THE STONE AGE FAMILY FROM VIKING LAND:
1 The Stones discover America 1975
2 The Stones explore Britain 1975

Althea
DESMOND THE DINOSAUR:
1 Desmond the dinosaur 1974
2 Desmond goes to school 1974
3 Desmond the dusty dinosaur 1974
4 Desmond and the monsters 1975
5 Desmond goes to New York 1975
6 Desmond and the stranger 1976
7 Desmond goes to Scotland 1977
8 Desmond goes boating 1977
9 Desmond at the carnival 1978
10 Desmond and the fancy dress party 1979
11 Desmond the Dinosaur storybook 1980
12 Desmond at the zoo 1981
13 The adventures of Desmond Dinosaur 1981
14 Desmond starts school 1982

□

1 Jeremy Mouse 1973
2 Jeremy Mouse and the cat 1980
3 Jeremy Mouse was hungry 1981

□

1 Gingerbread band 1974
2 Gingerbread men 1975

Ambrus, Victor
1 Dracula: Everything you always wanted to know but were too afraid to ask 1980
2 Dracula's bedtime storybook: Tales to keep you awake at night 1981

Anderson, Verily
THE YORK FAMILY SERIES:
1 Vanload to Venice 1961
2 Nine times never 1962
3 The Yorks in London 1964

BROWNIES SERIES:
1 Amanda and the Brownies 1962
2 The Brownies and the golden hand 1963
3 The Brownies day abroad 1964
4 The Brownies and the ponies 1965
5 The Brownies on wheels 1966
6 The Brownies and their animal friends 1967
7 The Brownies cook-book 1975
8 The Brownies camp fire cook book 1976
9 The Brownies and the christening 1977
10 The Brownies and the wedding day 1980

Andreus, Hans
1 Stories of Mr Bumblemoose 1970
2 Mr Bumblemoose and the flying boy 1971
3 Mr Bumblemoose and the glad dog 1972
4 Mr Bumblemoose and the mumblepuss 1973
5 Mr Bumblemoose buys a motor car 1973
6 Mr Bumblemoose and the laughing record 1974
7 Mr Bumblemoose and the tiger skin rug 1975
8 Mr Bumblemoose goes to Paris 1975
'Mr Bumblemoose Omnibus' 1977 contains 2, 3, 5.

Andrews, Stephen

1 Cubs with a difference 1973
2 Cubs away 1974
3 Cubs on Saturday 1976
4 Cubs at play 1977
5 Cubs ahoy 1979

Andrew, Prudence

1 Ginger over the wall 1962
2 Ginger and Batty Billy 1963
3 Ginger and No. 10 1964
4 Ginger among the pigeons 1966

Anglund, Joan Walsh

COWBOY SERIES:
1 The brave cowboy 1959
2 Cowboy and his friend 1961
3 Cowboy's secret life 1964
4 The Cowboy's Christmas 1973

Anno, Mitsumasa

1 Anno's alphabet 1974
2 Anno's counting book 1977
3 Anno's journey 1978
4 Anno's Italy 1979
5 Anno's animals 1979
6 King's flower 1980
7 Anno's medieval world 1980
8 Anno's magical ABC and Anomorphic alphabet 1981
9 Anno's Britain 1981
10 Anno's counting house 1982
11 Anno's mysterious multiplying jar 1983
12 Anno's USA 1983

Anson, Brian

1 Gus and Gilly 1969
2 Gus and Gilly: the winter journey 1969

Antrobus, John

1 Ronnie and the great knitted robbery 1982
2 Ronnie and the haunted Rolls Royce 1982

Appiah, Peggy

1 Tales of an Ashanti father 1967
2 The Pineapple child and other tales from Ashanti 1969
3 Why the hyena does not care for fish and other tales from the Ashanti gold weights 1977

Appleton, Victor II

1 Tom Swift and his outpost in space 1969
2 Tom Swift and his giant robot 1969
3 Tom Swift and his 3-d telejector 1969
4 Tom Swift and his race to the moon 1969
5 Tom Swift and his automatic tracker 1969
6 Tom Swift and the captive planetoid 1969
7 Tom Swift and the cosmic astronauts 1969
8 Tom Swift and the visitor from planet X 1969
9 Tom Swift and the asteroid pirates 1969
10 Tom Swift and his sonic boom trap 1969
11 Tom Swift and his sub-ocean geotron 1969
12 Tom Swift and the mystery comet 1969
13 Tom Swift and his triphibian atomicar 1970
14 Tom Swift and his dyna 4 capsule 1970
15 Tom Swift and his megascope space prober 1970
16 Tom Swift and his repelatron skyway 1970
17 Tom Swift and his polar-ray dynasphere 1970
18 Tom Swift and his G-force inverter 1970
19 Tom Swift and the phantom satellite 1971
20 Tom Swift and his cosmotron express 1971

Apsley, Brenda

1 Leo goes on a plane 1978
2 Leo goes on a ship 1978
3 Leo goes on a train 1978

Ardizzone, Edward

1 Little Tim and the brave sea captain 1936
2 Tim and Lucy go to sea 1938
3 Tim to the rescue 1949
4 Tim and Charlotte 1951
5 Tim in danger 1953
6 Tim all alone 1956
7 Tim's friend Towser 1962
8 Tim and Ginger 1965
9 Tim to the lighthouse 1968
10 Tim's last voyage 1972
11 Ship's cook Ginger 1977

Arkle, Phyllis

1 Roddy and roadman 1970
2 Roddy and the rustlers 1972
3 Roddy on the motorway 1974
4 Roddy on the canal 1975
5 Roddy and the puma 1979
6 Roddy and the miniature railway 1980
□
1 A village dinosaur 1970
2 Two village dinosaurs 1971

Arthur, Ruth Mabel

1 Carolina's holiday and other stories 1957
2 Carolina's golden bird and other stories 1958
3 Carolina and Roberto 1961
4 Carolina and the sea-horse and other stories 1964

CROOKED BROWNIE SERIES:

1 The crooked Brownie 1936
2 The crooked Brownie in town 1942
3 The crooked Brownie at the seaside 1942

Arthur, Robert *see* **Hitchcock, Alfred, Three Investigators series**

Arundel, Honor

EMMA SERIES:

1 The high house 1966
2 Emma's island 1968
3 Emma in love 1970
□
1 The terrible temptation 1971
2 The blanket word 1973

Atkinson, Mary Evelyn

THE LOCKETT FAMILY SERIES:

1 August adventure 1936
2 Mystery manor 1937
3 The compass points north 1938
4 Smugglers' gap 1939
5 Going gangster 1940
6 Crusoe Island 1941
7 Challenge to adventure 1942
8 The monster of Widgeon Weir 1943
9 The nest of the scarecrow 1944
10 Problem party 1945
11 Chimney cottage 1946
12 House on the moor 1947
13 The thirteenth adventure 1948
14 Steeple folly 1950

Augarde, Steve

1 Barnaby Shrew goes to sea 1978
2 Barnaby Shrew, Black Dan and the Mighty Wedgewood 1979

Avery, Gillian

1 The warden's neice 1957
2 The Italian spring 1964
3 Trespassers at Charlecote 1958
4 James without Thomas 1959
5 The Elephant War 1960
1 and 2 are direct sequels but characters recur in others, particularly members of the Smith family.
□
1 Ellen's birthday 1971
2 Ellen and the queen 1972
3 Ellen and the snowy white pinny

Awdry, Rev. Wilbert Vere

1 The three railway engines 1945
2 Thomas the tank engine 1946
3 James the red engine 1947
4 Tank engine Thomas again 1948
5 Troublesome engines 1949
6 Henry the green engine 1950
7 Toby the tram engine 1951
8 Gordon the big engine 1952
9 Edward the blue engine 1953
10 Four little engines 1954
11 Percy the small engine 1955
12 Eight famous engines 1957
13 Duck and diesel engine 1957
14 Little old engine 1958
15 The twin engines 1959
16 Branch line engines 1960
17 Gallant old engine 1961
18 Very old engines 1961
19 Stepney the "Bluebell" engine 1962
20 Mountain engines 1963
21 Main line engines 1966
22 Small railway engines 1967
23 Enterprising engines 1968
24 Oliver the Western engine 1969
25 Duke the lost engine 1971
26 Tramway engine 1973

B.B., *pseud.* **[D.J. Watkins-Pritchford]**

BILL BADGER SERIES:

1 Bill Badger and the wandering wind
2 Bill Badger's winter cruise 1959
3 Bill Badger and the pirates 1960
4 Bill Badger's finest hour 1961
5 Bill Badger's whispering reeds adventure 1962
6 Bill Badger's big mistake 1963
7 Bill Badger's last adventure
8 Bill Badger and the big store robbery 1967
9 Bill Badger's voyage to the world's end 1969

□

1 The little grey men 1942
2 Little grey men go down the bright stream 1948

□

1 The Forest of Boland Light Railway 1955
2 The Wizard of Boland 1959

□

1 Monty Woodpig and his bubblebuzz car 1958
2 Monty Woodpig's caravan 1957

Baker, Alan

1 Benjamin and the box 1977
2 Benjamin bounces back 1978
3 Benjamin's dreadful dream 1980
4 Benjamin's book 1982

Baker, Jeannie

1 Grandfather 1977
2 Grandmother 1978

Baker, Margaret Joyce

THREE BEARS SERIES:

1 The shoe shop bears 1964
2 Hannibal and the bears 1965
3 Bears back in business 1967
4 Hi-jinks joins the bears 1968
5 Teabag and the bears 1970
6 Boots and the ginger bears 1972

THE RIDLEY FAMILY:

1 Castaway Christmas 1963
2 Cut off from the crumpets 1964
3 Sand in our shoes 1976

HOMER SERIES:

1 Nonsense! said the tortoise 1949
2 Homer sees the Queen 1956
3 Homer goes to Stratford 1958
4 Homer in orbit 1961
5 Homer goes west 1965

Ball, Brian

1 Jackson's house 1974
2 Jackson's friend 1975
3 Jackson's holiday 1977
4 Jackson and the magpies 1978

Ballantyne, Robert Michael

1 The coral island 1858
2 The gorilla hunters 1861

□

1 Sunk at sea; or the adventures of Wandering Will in the Pacific 1869
2 Lost in the forest; or Wandering Will's adventure in South America 1869
3 Over the Rocky Mountains; or Wandering Will in the land of the Red Skin 1869

Ballard, Martin

1 Benjie's portion 1969
2 Speaking drums of Ashanti 1970

2 is about Simon, the son of Benjie.

Bancroft, John, *pseud.* **[Alan Charles Jenkins]**

JAMES STEEL:

1 Guardians of honour 1961
2 The ring of truth 1962

Banner, Angela

1 Ant and bee 1950
2 More Ant and Bee 1956
3 One Two Three with Ant and Bee 1958
4 Around the world with Ant and Bee 1960
5 More and more Ant and Bee 1960
6 Ant and Bee and the rainbow 1962
7 Ant and Bee and the Kind Dog 1963
8 Happy birthday with Ant and Bee 1964
9 Ant and Bee and the ABC 1966
10 Ant and Bee time 1969
11 Ant and Bee and the secret 1970
12 Ant and Bee big buy bag 1971
13 Ant and Bee and the doctor 1971
14 Ant and Bee go shopping 1972

Bannerman, Helen

1 Story of little Black Sambo 1899
2 Story of Sambo and the twins 1937

Barklem, Jill

BRAMBLY HEDGE SERIES:
1 Spring story 1980
2 Summer story 1980
3 Autumn story 1980
4 Winter story 1980
5 Secret staircase 1983
'The Big Book of Brambly Hedge' 1981 contains the first four stories.

Barne, Kitty

ROSINA SERIES:
1 Rosina Copper the mystery mare 1954
2 Rosina and son 1956
FARRAR FAMILY SERIES:
1 Family footlights 1939
2 Visitors from London 1940
3 Dusty's windmill 1949

Barratt, Isabel

1 The adventures of Rosa 1979
2 Bardolph the beastly beagle 1979

Barrie, Alexander

JONATHAN KANE SERIES:
1 Fly for three lives 1975
2 Operation midnight 1975
3 Let them all starve 1975
4 Jonathan Kane's jungle adventure 1977
5 Jonathan Kane climbs high 1977

Barry, Margaret Stuart

1 Woozy 1973
2 A Woozy gets lost 1973
3 The Woozies go to school 1973
4 Woozies on television 1973
5 Woozy and the weightwatchers 1976
6 Woozies hold a frubarb week 1976
7 The monster in Woozy garden 1976
8 The Woozies go visiting 1976
□
1 Tommy Mac 1972
2 Tommy Mac battles on 1974
3 Tommy Mac on safari 1975
□
1 Maggie Gumption 1979
2 Maggie Gumption flies high 1981
□
1 Boffy and the teacher-eater 1973
2 Boffy and the Mumford ghosts 1974
□
1 Simon and the witch 1976
2 The return of the witch 1978
3 The witch on Monopoly Manor 1979
4 The witch on holiday 1983

Batchelor, Mary

PEG AND JAMES SERIES:
1 Peg and James plant some bulbs 1977
2 Peg and James and the new baby 1977
3 Peg and James go to market 1977
4 Peg and James go to the park 1977

Baum, Lyman Frank

1 The wonderful wizard of Oz 1900
2 The marvelous land of Oz 1904
3 Ozma of Oz 1906
4 Dorothy and the wizard of Oz 1908
5 The road to Oz 1909
6 The emerald city of Oz 1910
7 The patchwork girl of Oz 1913
8 Tik-Tok of Oz 1914
9 The scarecrow of Oz 1915
10 Rinkitink of Oz 1916
11 The lost princess of Oz 1917
12 The tin woodman of Oz 1918
13 The magic of Oz 1919
14 Glinda of Oz 1920
There are many other titles by different authors, but not published in UK.

Baumann, Hans

AMERICA-ASIA-AFRICA TRILOGY:
1 Son of Columbus 1957
2 Sons of the steppe 1957
3 The barque of the brothers 1958

Baumann, K. *and* **McKee, David**

1 Joachim the dustman 1974
2 Joachim the policeman 1975

Bawden, Nina

THE MALLORY CHILDREN:
1 The secret passage 1963
2 On the run 1964
CARRIE WILLOW STORIES:
1 Carrie's war 1973
2 Rebel on a rock 1978

Baxter, Gillian

1 Jump to the stars 1961
2 The difficult summer 1962
3 The perfect horse 1963
□
1 Pantomime ponies 1969
2 Save the ponies 1971
3 Ponies by the sea 1974
4 Ponies in harness 1977
5 Special delivery 1977
6 Tan and Tarmac 1980

Bayley, Viola

ADVENTURE SERIES:
1 Paris adventure 1954
2 Lebanon adventure 1955
3 Kashmir adventure 1956
4 Corsican adventure 1956
5 Turkish adventure 1957
6 London adventure 1962
7 Swedish adventure 1963
8 Italian adventure 1964
9 Scottish adventure 1964
10 Welsh adventure 1966
11 Austrian adventure 1968
12 Jersey adventure 1969
13 Adriatic adventure 1970
14 Caribbean adventure 1971
Not sequels, but characters recur in many of the volumes.

Beaman, Sydney George Hulme

TOYTOWN SERIES:
1 The road to Toytown 1925
2 The wooden knight 1925
3 Tales of Toytown 1928
4 The tale of Captain Brass, the pirate 1928
5 Tales of the inventor 1928
6 The tale of the magician 1928
7 Wireless in Toytown 1930
8 The Toytown book 1930
9 Ernest the policeman 1930
10 The Toytown mystery 1932
11 Stories from Toytown 1938
12 Mr Noah's holiday 1942
13 Dirty work at the Dog and Whistle 1942
14 The brave deed of Ernest the Policeman 1942
15 Golf (Toytown rules) 1943
16 Frightfulness in the Theatre Royal 1943
17 Larry the lamb 1946
18 Tea for two *and* A portrait of the mayor 1957
19 Ernest the brave *and* The Toytown mystery 1957
20 The mayor's sea voyage 1958
21 The Theatre Royal *and* Punch and Judy 1958
22 Toytown goes west 1958
23 The enchanted ark 1958
24 The disgraceful business at Mrs Goose's 1958
25 Larry the plumber 1961
26 The Toytown treasure 1961
27 The conversion of Mr Growser 1961
28 The great Toytown war 1961
29 How the radio came to Toytown 1961
30 Pistols for two 1962
31 A Christmas Toytown party 1962
32 Mr Growser moves house 1963
33 Dreadful doings in Ark Street 1963
34 The Arkville dragon 1963
35 The showing up of Larry the lamb 1963
36 The Toytown pantomime 1963

Beckman, Gunnel

1 Mia 1974
2 The loneliness of Mia 1975

Belloc, Hilaire

1 The bad child's book of beasts 1896
2 More beasts (for worse children) 1897
□
1 Cautionary tales for children 1907
2 New cautionary tales 1930
Collections of verse.

Bemelmans, Ludvig

1 Madeline 1952
2 Madeline's rescue 1953
3 Madeline's Christmas in Texas 1955
4 Madeline and the bad hat 1958
5 Madeline and the gypsies 1959
6 Madeline in London 1962

Benedict, Rex

THE PECOS GANG:
1 Good luck Arizona man 1973
2 Goodbye to the purple sage 1974
3 Last stand at Goodbye Gulch 1975
4 The ballad of Cactus Jack 1976
4 is a direct sequel of 2.

Bentley, Anne

1 Groggs have a wonderful summer 1980
2 Groggs' day out 1981

Berenstain, Jan *and* Stan

THE BERENSTAIN BEARS SERIES:

1 The big honey hunt 1966
2 The bike lesson 1967
3 The bear scouts 1968
4 Inside outside, upside down 1969
5 Bears' Christmas 1969
6 Bears' holiday 1969
7 Bears on wheels 1970
8 Old hat, new hat 1971
9 The B. Book 1972
10 Bears in the night 1972
11 The bears' picnic 1973
12 He bear, she bear 1975
13 The bear detectives 1977
14 Berenstain bears and the spooky old tree 1979
15 Berenstain bears and the missing dinosaur bone 1980
16 Bears' activity book 1981
17 Berenstain bears and the sitter 1982
18 Berenstain bears go to school 1982
19 Berenstain bears go to the doctor 1982
20 Berenstain bears' moving day 1982
21 Berenstain bears visit the dentist 1982
22 The bears' new baby 1975
23 Berenstain bears' nursery tales 1974

'The Bears' almanac', a collection of stories.
'The Bears' nature guide' 1977, 'The Berenstain Bears' science fair' 1978 – non fiction.

Beresford, Elizabeth

GARY, JIM AND JANE SERIES:

1 Television mystery 1957
2 Flying doctor mystery 1958
3 Trouble at Tullington Castle 1958
4 Gappy goes West 1959
5 The Tullington Film-makers 1960
6 Strange hiding place 1962
7 The missing formula mystery 1963
8 Flying doctor to the rescue 1964
9 Game set and match 1965
10 The black mountain mystery 1967

□

1 The honeysuckle line 1960
2 Danger on the old pull 'n' push 1962

□

1 The Wombles 1968
2 The wandering Wombles 1970
3 The Wombles at work 1973
4 The invisible Womble and other stories 1973
5 The Wombles in danger 1973
6 Wombles to the rescue 1974
7 The Wombles go to the seaside 1974
8 The Wombles' gift book 1975
9 The Wombles make a clean sweep 1975
10 The Wombles go round the world 1976
11 The world of the Wombles 1976
12 Wombling free 1978

'The Wombles of Wimbledon' 1976 is an omnibus of 3 and 6. 7 contains five new stories and other items.

LITTLE WOMBLES:

1 The snow Womble 1975
2 Orinoco runs away 1975
3 Tomsk and the tired tree 1975
4 Wellington and the blue balloon 1975
5 Bungo knows best 1976
6 The MacWomble's pipe band 1976
7 Madame Cholet's picnic party 1976
8 Tobermory's big surprise 1976

A miniature series for younger children.

Berg, Leila

1 The adventures of Chunky 1950
2 Trust Chunky 1954

□

1 The little car 1972
2 The little car has a day out 1973

Bergstrom, Gunilla

1 Alfie and his secret friend 1979
2 Alfie and the monster 1979
3 Who'll save Alfie Atkins? 1979
4 You're a sly one, Alfie Atkins 1979

Bermingham, Iris

1 Hapi and the Morepork 1974
2 Hapi and the forbidden island 1978

Berna, Paul

1 Threshold of the stars 1958
2 Continent in the sky 1959

GABY SERIES:

1 A hundred million francs 1957

2 The street musician 1960
3 The mystery of Saint-Salgue 1963
4 Gaby and the new money fraud 1971

□

1 Vagabonds of the Pacific 1973
2 The vagabonds ashore 1973

□

1 The clue of the black cat 1964
2 The mule of the motorway 1967
3 A truckload of rice 1968

Berrisford, Judith Mary

1 Skipper, the dog from the sea 1955
2 Skipper and the headland four 1957
3 Skipper's exciting summer 1958
4 Skipper and the runaway boy 1960
5 Skipper and son 1961

□

1 Taff the sheepdog 1949
2 Son of Taff 1959
3 S.O.S. for sheepdog Taff 1963
4 Taff and the stolen ponies 1965

JACKIE AND BABS SERIES:

1 Jackie won a pony 1958
2 Ten ponies and Jackie 1959
3 Jackie's pony patrol 1961
4 Jackie and the pony trekkers 1963
5 Jackie's pony camp summer 1968
6 Jackie and the pony boys 1970
7 Jackie's show jumping surprise 1973
8 Jackie and the misfit pony 1976
9 Jackie on pony island 1977
10 Jackie and the pony thieves 1978
11 Jackie and the phantom ponies 1979
12 Jackie and the moonlight pony 1980
13 Jackie and the pony rivals 1981
14 Jackie and the missing showjumper 1982
15 Change ponies Jackie 1983

THE BROOKE FAMILY SERIES:

1 A pony in the family 1959
2 A colt in the family 1962
3 A showjumper in the family 1964

□

1 Pony trekkers go home 1982
2 Sabotage at Stableways 1982

Beskow, Elsa Maartman

1 Aunt Green, Aunt Brown and Aunt Lavender 1918
2 Aunt Brown's birthday 1925
3 The adventures of Peter and Lotta 1929

Best, Herbert

1 Desmond's first case 1961
2 Desmond the dog detective 1962
3 Desmond and the peppermint ghost 1965
4 Desmond and dog Friday 1968

Best, Jacqueline

PAUL AND FRITZI'S YEAR:

1 Spring 1972
2 Summer 1972
3 Autumn 1972
4 Winter 1972

Bexall, Eva

1 Minister's naughty grandchildren 1978
2 Christmas with grandfather 1979

Bidmead, Christopher *see* **Dr Who series**

Bidwell, Dafne

1 The tiger gang and the hijackers 1977
2 The tiger gang and the car thieves 1979

Biegel, Paul

1 The little captain 1973
2 The little captain and the seven towers 1974
3 The little captain and the pirate treasure 1980

□

1 The dwarfs of Nosegay 1978
2 The fattest dwarf of Nosegay 1980
3 Virgil Nosegay and the cake hunt 1981
4 Virgil Nosegay and the Hopmobile 1983

Bird, Kenneth

1 A dog called Himself 1968
2 Himself and MacCafferty's queen 1969
3 Stardom for Himself 1970
4 Himself in a yellow balloon 1971
5 Himself and a missing uncle 1972
6 Not a word for Himself 1973
7 Himself and Whistler's niece 1974
8 Himself and the Rooney rebellion 1975
9 Himself and the Kerry crusher 1976
10 Himself beats the bill 1977
11 Himself and the fake santas 1978
12 Himself and tomorrow's ogre 1978
13 Himself and the golden ghost 1979

Bird, Maria

1 Andy Pandy and his hobby horse 1953
2 Andy Pandy and the gingerbread man 1953
3 Andy Pandy's washing day 1953
4 Andy Pandy's nursery rhymes 1954
5 Andy Pandy and the ducklings 1954
6 Andy Pandy's tea party 1954
7 Andy Pandy's jumping up book 1954
8 Andy Pandy in the country 1955
9 Andy Pandy's jack in the box 1955
10 Andy Pandy's shop 1955
11 Andy Pandy and Teddy at the zoo 1956
12 Andy Pandy and the white kitten 1956
13 Andy Pandy and the willow tree 1956
14 Andy Pandy builds a house for Looby Loo 1956
15 Andy Pandy's kite 1957
16 Andy Pandy paints his house 1958
17 Andy Pandy's shopping bag 1958
18 Andy Pandy and the hedgehog 1959
19 Andy Pandy's puppy 1960
20 Andy Pandy and the woolly lamb 1960
21 Andy Pandy and the teddy dog 1960
22 Andy Pandy's dovecote 1960
23 Andy Pandy and the baby pigs 1961
24 Andy Pandy's little goat 1961
25 Andy Pandy and the patchwork cat 1962
26 Andy Pandy and the snowman 1962
27 Andy Pandy's new pet 1963
28 Andy Pandy's weather house 1963
29 Andy Pandy plays lions and tigers 1964
30 Andy Pandy's playhouse 1964
31 Andy Pandy and the green puppy 1965
32 Andy Pandy and the badger 1965
33 Andy Pandy and the scarecrow 1966
34 Andy Pandy's red motor car 1967
35 Andy Pandy and the yellow dog 1968
36 Andy Pandy and the spotted cow 1971
37 Andy Pandy and the baby monkey 1972
38 Andy Pandy and the tiny piglet 1972

Biro, Val

1 Gumdrop; the adventures of a vintage car 1966
2 Gumdrop and the farmer's friend 1967
3 Gumdrop on the rally 1968
4 Gumdrop on the move 1969
5 Gumdrop goes to London 1971
6 Gumdrop finds a friend 1973
7 Gumdrop in double trouble 1975
8 Gumdrop and the steam roller 1976
9 Gumdrop posts a letter 1976
10 Gumdrop on the Brighton run 1976
11 Gumdrop has a birthday 1977
12 Gumdrop gets his wings 1979
13 Gumdrop finds a ghost 1980
14 Gumdrop and the secret switches 1981
15 Gumdrop makes a start 1982
16 Gumdrop goes to school 1983
17 Gumdrop gets a lift 1983
18 Gumdrop at the zoo 1983
19 Gumdrop in a hurry 1983

Bisset, Donald

1 Yak and the painted cave 1971
2 Yak and the seashell 1971
3 Yak and the buried treasure 1972
4 Yak and the ice cream 1972
5 Yak goes home 1973
6 The adventures of Yak 1978

□

1 Johnny here and there 1981
2 Johnny the tin tortoise 1982

□

1 Talks with Tiger 1967
2 Tiger wants more 1971
3 "Oh dear", said Tiger 1975

Black, Cindy

1 Mojo Swoptops gets all mixed up 1979
2 Mojo Swoptops keeps his cool 1979
3 Mojo Swoptops cleans up 1979
4 Mojo Swoptops goes to the races 1979
5 Mojo Swoptops fights a fire 1979
6 Mojo Swoptops goes to school 1979

Blake, Justin

GARRY HALLIDAY SERIES:

1 Garry Halliday and the disappearing diamonds 1960
2 Garry Halliday and the ray of death 1961
3 Garry Halliday and the kidnapped five 1962
4 Garry Halliday and the sands of time 1963
5 Garry Halliday and the flying foxes 1965

Blathwayt, Jean

1 Lucy's Brownie road 1971
2 Lucy's last Brownie challenge 1972

Blishen, Edward *see* **Garfield, Leon** *and* **Blishen, Edward**

Block, Bob
1 Rentaghost 1982
2 Rentaghost unlimited 1982

Bloomfield, Frena
THE DARKWORLD LEGENDS:
1 The dragon paths 1973
2 Earthrise 1973
3 Mindmaster 1973
4 The Plains of darkworld 1973
5 Sky fleet of Atlantis 1973

Blume, Judy
1 Tales of a fourth grade nothing 1979
2 Superfudge 1980

Blyton, Enid
1 The adventures of Pip 1948
2 More adventures of Pip 1948
□
1 The children at Happy-House 1946
2 The Happy-House children again 1947
3 Happy-House children 1966
FAMOUS FIVE SERIES:
1 Five on a Treasure Island 1942
2 Five go adventuring again 1943
3 Five run away together 1944
4 Five go to Smuggler's Top 1945
5 Five go off in a caravan 1946
6 Five on Kirrin Island again 1947
7 Five go off to camp 1948
8 Five get into trouble 1949
9 Five fall into adventure 1950
10 Five on a hike together 1951
11 Five have a wonderful time 1952
12 Five go down to the sea 1953
13 Five go to Mystery Moor 1954
14 Five have plenty of fun 1955
15 Five on a secret trail 1956
16 Five go to Billycock Hill 1957
17 Five get into a fix 1958
18 Five on Finniston Farm 1960
19 Five go to Demon's rocks 1961
10 Five have a mystery to solve 1962
21 Five are together again 1963
See also **Voilier,** TV adventures of Famous Five.
BARNEY SERIES:
1 The Rockingdown mystery 1949
2 The Rilloby Fair mystery 1950
3 The Rubadub mystery 1952
4 The Ring o' bells mystery 1955
5 The Rat-o-tat mystery 1956
6 The Ragamuffin mystery 1959
FARAWAY TREE SERIES:
1 Enchanted wood 1939
2 Magic faraway tree 1943
3 Folk of the faraway tree 1946
4 Up the faraway tree 1951
□
1 Caravan family 1953
2 Run-about holidays 1955
3 Four in a family 1956
MALORY TOWERS SERIES:
1 First term at Malory Towers 1946
2 Second form at Malory Towers 1947
3 Third year at Malory Towers 1948
4 Upper fourth at Malory Towers 1949
5 In the fifth at Malory Towers 1950
6 Last term at Malory Towers 1951
□
1 Island of adventure 1944
2 Castle of adventure 1946
3 Valley of adventure 1947
4 Sea of adventure 1948
5 Mountain of adventure 1949
6 Ship of adventure 1950
7 Circus of adventure 1952
8 River of adventure 1955
□
1 Adventures of the Wishing-Chair 1937
2 The Wishing-Chair again 1950
□
1 Naughty Amelia Jane! 1939
2 Amelia Jane again 1946
3 More about Amelia Jane 1954
□
1 The adventurous four 1941
2 The adventurous four again 1947
FIVE FIND-OUTERS:
1 Mystery of the burnt cottage 1943
2 Mystery of the disappearing cat 1944
3 Mystery of the secret room 1945
4 Mystery of the spiteful letters 1946
5 Mystery of the missing necklace 1947
6 Mystery of the hidden house 1948
7 Mystery of the pantomime cat 1949
8 Mystery of the invisible thief 1950
9 Mystery of the vanished prince 1951
10 Mystery of the strange bundle 1952

11 Mystery of Holly Lane 1953
12 Mystery of Tally-Ho cottage 1954
13 Mystery of the missing man 1956
14 Mystery of the strange messages 1957
15 Mystery of the Banshee Towers 1961

NAUGHTIEST GIRL SERIES:

1 Naughtiest girl in the school 1940
2 Naughtiest girl again 1942
3 Naughtiest girl is a monitor 1945

NODDY SERIES:

1 Noddy goes to Toyland 1949
2 Hurrah for little Noddy 1950
3 Noddy and his car 1951
4 Noddy has a shock 1951
5 Noddy has more adventures 1951
6 A tale of little Noddy 1951
7 Noddy goes to the seaside 1951
8 Here comes Noddy again! 1951
9 Noddy off to Rockinghorse land 1951
10 Noddy's house of books 1951
11 Noddy and Big Ears have a picnic 1951
12 Noddy and Big Ears 1952
13 Noddy and the witch's wand 1952
14 Noddy's colour strip book 1952
15 Noddy goes to school 1952
16 Noddy's ark of books 1952
17 Noddy's car gets a squeak 1952
18 Noddy's penny wheel car 1952
19 Well done Noddy 1952
20 Noddy and the cuckoo's nest 1953
21 Noddy at the seaside 1953
22 Noddy gets captured 1953
23 Noddy is very silly 1953
24 Noddy's garage of books 1953
25 How funny you are, Noddy 1954
26 Noddy and the magic rubber 1955
27 Noddy's castle of books 1954
28 Noddy gets into trouble 1954
29 You funny little Noddy 1955
30 Noddy meets Father Christmas 1955
31 Noddy in Toyland 1955
32 Noddy and the Tessie Bear 1956
33 The Noddy toy station books 1956
34 Be brave little Noddy 1956
35 Noddy and his friends 1956
36 A day with little Noddy 1956
37 Noddy and the bumpy dog 1957
38 Do look out, Noddy! 1957
39 You're a good friend, Noddy! 1957
40 Noddy has an adventure 1958
41 The Noddy shop book 1958
42 Noddy's own nursery rhymes 1959
43 Noddy's car picture book 1959
44 Noddy goes to sea 1959
45 Noddy and Bunky 1959
46 Noddy goes to the fair 1960
47 Cheer up little Noddy 1960
48 Mr Plod and little Noddy 1961
49 Noddy and the Tootles 1962
50 A day at school with Noddy 1962
51 Noddy and the aeroplane 1964
52 Noddy's treasure box 1965
53 Noddy and his passengers 1967
54 Noddy and the magic boots 1967
55 Noddy's funny kite 1967
56 Noddy goes to market 1976
57 Noddy's busy day 1977

There are several other Noddy books—'The big book of Noddy', six volumes, 'Noddy's tall blue book' (also green, orange, pink, red, and yellow books), and several painting and cut-out books under various titles.

□

1 Mister Meddle's mischief 1940
2 Mister Meddle's muddles 1950
3 Merry Mister Meddle 1954

□

1 Mr Pinkwhistle interferes 1950
2 The adventures of Mr Pinkwhistle 1941
3 Mr Pinkwhistle's party 1955
4 Mr Pinkwhistle's big book 1958

SECRET SEVEN SERIES:

1 The Secret Seven 1949
2 Secret Seven adventure 1950
3 Well done Secret Seven 1951
4 Secret Seven on the trail 1952
5 Go ahead Secret Seven 1953
6 Good work, Secret Seven 1954
7 Secret Seven win through 1955
8 Three cheers Secret Seven 1956
9 Secret Seven mystery 1957
10 Puzzle for the Secret Seven 1958
11 Secret Seven and the fireworks 1959
12 Shock for the Secret Seven 1961
13 Good old Secret Seven 1960
14 Look out Secret Seven 1962
15 Fun for the Secret Seven 1963

□

1 Six cousins at Mistletoe Farm 1948
2 Six cousins again 1950

ST. CLARE'S SERIES:

1 Twins at St. Clare's 1941

2 O'Sullivan twins 1942
3 Summer term at St. Clare's 1943
4 Second form at St. Clare's 1944
5 Claudine at St. Clare's 1944
6 Fifth form at St. Clare's 1954

Boden, Hilda

NOEL SERIES:

1 Noel and the donkeys 1960
2 Noel's happy day 1961
3 Noel's Christmas holidays 1962
4 Noel the brave 1963
5 Noel the explorer 1965
6 A job for Noel 1966

□

1 Joanna's special pony 1960
2 Joanna rides the hills 1961

Bond, Michael

1 A bear called Paddington 1958
2 More about Paddington 1959
3 Paddington helps out 1960
4 Paddington abroad 1961
5 Paddington at large 1962
6 Paddington marches on 1964
7 Paddington at work 1966
8 Paddington goes to town 1968
9 Paddington takes the air 1970
10 Paddington on top 1974
11 Paddington takes the test 1979

PADDINGTON PICTURE BOOKS:

1 Paddington Bear 1972
2 Paddington's garden 1972
3 Paddington at the circus 1973
4 Paddington goes shopping 1973
5 Paddington at the seaside 1975
6 Paddington at the tower 1975
7 Paddington at the station 1976
8 Paddington goes to the sales 1976
9 Paddington takes a bath 1976
10 Paddington's new room 1976
11 Paddington does it himself 1977
12 Paddington in the kitchen 1977
13 Paddington hits out 1977
14 Paddington's birthday party 1977

□

1 Here comes Thursday 1969
2 Thursday rides again 1968
3 Thursday ahoy 1969
4 Thursday in Paris 1971

□

1 Tales of Olga da Polga 1972
2 Olga da Polga meets her match 1973
3 Olga da Polga 1975
4 Olga carries on 1976
5 Olga takes charge 1982

Boshell, Gordon

1 Captain Cobwebb 1967
2 Captain Cobwebb's cowboy 1969
3 Captain Cobwebb's cobra 1971
4 Captain Cobwebb's adventures 1973
5 Captain Cobwebb and the red transistor 1974
6 Captain Cobwebb and the Crustaks 1975
7 Captain Cobwebb and the Chinese unicorn 1975
8 Captain Cobwebb and the quogs 1977
9 Captain Cobwebb and the mischief man 1977
10 Captain Cobwebb and the magic drops 1978
11 Captain Cobwebb and the amazing cloud 1979

THE SECRET GUARDIANS SERIES:

1 The black Mercedes 1975
2 The million pound ransom 1975
3 The Mendip money makers 1976

Boston, Lucy Maria

GREEN KNOWE SERIES:

1 Children of Green Knowe 1954
2 The chimneys of Green Knowe 1958
3 The river at Green Knowe 1959
4 A stranger at Green Knowe 1961
5 An enemy at Green Knowe 1964
6 The guardians of the house 1974
7 The stones of Green Knowe 1976

6 is a short fantasy of the future when Green Knowe is empty. 'The house that grew' 1972, is a picture book story based on Green Knowe. 'Memory in a house' 1973, is the true story of the house on which Green Knowe was based.

Boylston, Helen Dore

1 Carol goes on the stage 1943
2 Carol in repertory 1944
3 Carol comes to Broadway 1945
4 Carol on tour 1946

□

1 Sue Barton, student nurse 1939
2 Sue Barton, senior nurse 1940
3 Sue Barton, visiting nurse 1941

4 Sue Barton, rural nurse 1942
5 Sue Barton, superintendent nurse 1942
6 Sue Barton, neighbourhood nurse 1950
7 Sue Barton, staff nurse 1953

Brand, Christina
1 Nurse Matilda 1964
2 Nurse Matilda goes to town 1967
3 Nurse Matilda goes to hospital 1974

Brandenberg, Franz
EDWARD AND ELIZABETH SERIES:
1 A secret for grandmother's birthday 1976
2 No school today 1976
3 A robber! a robber! 1976
4 I don't feel well 1977
5 A picnic, hurrah! 1979
□
1 Leo and Emily 1982
2 Leo and Emily's big ideas 1982
FIELDMOUSE CHILDREN SERIES:
1 What can you make of it? 1979
2 Nice new neighbours 1979
3 Six new students 1979

Breinburg, Petronella
1 My brother Sean 1973
2 Doctor Sean 1974
3 Sean's red bike 1975
□
1 Sally-Ann's umbrella 1975
2 Sally-Ann in the snow 1977
3 Sally-Ann's skateboard 1979
4 Sally-Ann's party

Brenda, *pseud* **[Mrs Castle Smith]**
1 Froggy's little brother 1875
2 More about Froggy 1878

Brent-Dyer, E. M. *see* **Dyer, E. M. Brent**

Briggs, Raymond
1 Father Christmas 1974
2 Father Christmas goes on holiday 1975
'The Complete Father Christmas' 1978 contains both stories
□
1 Fungus the Bogeyman 1977
2 Fungus the Bogeyman plop-up book 1982
□
1 Gentleman Jim 1980
2 When the wind blows 1982
2 features the same characters as 1 but is an adult book.

Bright, Robert
1 Georgie 1945
2 Georgie to the rescue 1960
3 Georgie and the robbers 1964
4 Georgie and the magician 1967
5 Georgie's Hallowe'en 1972
6 Georgie and the noisy ghost 1973
7 Georgie goes West 1975
8 Georgie's Christmas card 1978
9 Georgie and the buried treasure 1981

Brinsmead, Hesba Fay
CLIPPIE NANCARROW:
1 Who calls from afar? 1971
2 Echo in the wilderness 1972
TRUELANCE FAMILY:
1 Longtime passing 1971
2 Longtime dreaming 1982

Brisley, Joyce Lankester
1 Milly-Molly-Mandy stories 1928
2 More of Milly-Molly-Mandy 1929
3 Further doings of Milly-Molly-Mandy 1932
4 Milly-Molly-Mandy again 1948
5 Milly-Molly-Mandy and Co. 1955
6 Milly-Molly-Mandy and Billy Bunt 1967

Brisville, Jean-Claude
1 Oleg, the snow leopard 1978
2 King Oleg 1982

Brogan, Mike
ACTION MAN:
1 The tough way out 1978
2 Counter attack 1978
3 Raid on Shuando! 1978
4 The spy trap 1978

Brook, Judy
1 Tim mouse 1966
2 The mouse and the major 1967
3 Tim mouse visits the farm 1968
4 Tim mouse goes down the stream 1969
5 Tim and Helen mouse 1970
6 Tim mouse and Father Christmas 1972

BELINDA BADGER:
1 Belinda 1976
2 Belinda and Father Christmas 1978
MRS NOAH:
1 Mrs Noah and the animals 1977
2 Mrs Noah's ABC, 123 1979

Brooke, L. L.
1 Johnny Crow's garden 1903
2 Johnny Crow's party 1906
3 Johnny Crow's new garden 1935

Brown, George Mackay
1 The two fiddlers 1974
2 Pictures in the cave 1977

Brown, H. D.
ANNA LAVINIA:
1 Beyond the paw paw trees 1956
2 The silver nutmeg 1957

Brown, Marc
1 Arthur's eyes 1982
2 The true Francine 1982
3 Arthur's April fool 1983

Brown, Mike
1 Animal fun ABC 1982
2 Animal fun 123 1982

Brown, Pamela
BLUE DOOR THEATRE SERIES:
1 Swish of the curtain 1941
2 Maddy alone 1945
3 Golden pavements 1947
4 Blue door venture 1949
5 Maddy again 1956

Brown, R. Haig-
1 Starbuck Valley winter 1944
2 Saltwater summer 1949

Brown, Roy
1 Amazon adventures of two children
2 Two children and their jungle
□
1 Flight of the sparrows
2 The white sparrow 1974

Browne, Anthony
1 Bear hunt, 1979
2 Bear goes to town 1982

Bruce, Dorita Fairlie
1 The senior prefect 1921
2 Dimsie moves up 1921
3 Dimsie moves up again 1922
4 Dimsie among the prefects 1923
5 Dimsie grows up 1924
6 Dimsie, head-girl 1925
7 Dimsie goes back 1927
8 Dimsie intervenes 1937
9 Dimsie carries on 1942
1 published as 'Dimsie goes to school' 1933.
□
1 The girls of St. Bride's 1923
2 The new girl and Nancy 1926
3 Nancy to the rescue 1927
4 Nancy at St. Bride's 1933
5 Nancy in the sixth 1935
6 Nancy returns to St. Bride's 1938
7 Nancy calls the tune 1944
6 also titled 'That boarding school girl'.
SPRINGDALE SERIES:
1 The new house-captain 1928
2 The best house in the school 1930
3 Captain of Springdale 1932
4 The new house at Springdale 1934
5 Prefects at Springdale 1938
6 Captain Anne 1939
□
1 Sally Scatterbrain 1956
2 Sally again 1959
3 Sally's summer term 1961

Bruce, Mary Grant
1 A little bush maid 1910
2 Mates at Billabong 1911
3 Norah of Billabong 1912
4 From Billabong to London 1915
5 Back to Billabong 1921
6 Billabong's daughter 1924
7 Billabong adventures 1927
8 Bill of Billabong 1931
9 Billabong's luck 1933
10 Wings above Billabong 1935
11 Billabong gold 1937
12 Son of Billabong 1939
13 Billabong riders 1952

Bruna, Dick
1 Miffy 1964
2 Miffy at the seaside 1964
3 Miffy at the zoo 1965

4 Miffy in the snow 1965
5 Miffy goes flying 1971
6 Miffy's birthday 1971
7 Miffy at the playground 1976
8 Miffy in hospital 1976
9 Miffy's dream 1979
□
1 Poppy Pig 1978
2 Poppy Pig's garden 1978

Buckeridge, Anthony

JENNINGS SERIES:

1 Jennings goes to school 1950
2 Jennings and Darbishire 1951
3 Jennings follows a clue 1952
4 Jennings' little hut 1953
5 Jennings' diary 1954
6 According to Jennings 1955
7 Our friend Jennings 1956
8 Thanks to Jennings 1957
9 Take Jennings for instance 1958
10 Jennings as usual 1959
11 The trouble with Jennings 1960
12 Just like Jennings 1962
13 Leave it to Jennings 1963
14 Jennings, of course 1964
15 Especially Jennings 1965
16 A bookful of Jennings 1966
17 Jennings abounding 1967
18 Jennings in particular 1968
19 Trust Jennings 1969
20 The Jennings report 1970
21 Typically Jennings 1971
22 Speaking of Jennings 1973
23 Jennings at large 1980
□
1 Rex Milligan's busy term 1954
2 Rex Milligan raises the roof 1955
3 Rex Milligan holds forth 1957
4 Rex Milligan reporting 1961

Buddee, Paul

AIR PATROL SERIES:

1 Air patrol and the hijackers 1973
2 Air patrol and the saboteurs 1973
3 Air patrol and the secret intruders 1973
4 Air patrol and the underwater spies 1973
□
1 Ann Rankin and the boy who painted horses 1972
2 Ann Rankin and the great flood 1973
3 Ann Rankin and the house on Coolabah Hill 1973
4 Ann Rankin and the lost valley 1973
□
1 Peter Devlin and the road bandits 1974
2 Peter Devlin buffalo hunter 1974
3 Peter Devlin fights for survival 1974
4 Peter Devlin, range rider 1974

Burch, T. T.

1 Shane McKellar and the face at the window 1979
2 Shane McKellar and the treasure hunt 1979

Burgess, Thornton Waldo

1 Old Mother West Wind 1910
2 Mother West Wind's children 1911
The above were re-issued in 1967.

Burgoyne, Peter *pseud.* **[Peter Burgoyne Rattenburg]**

1 The school of mystery 1954
2 The fighting formula 1956
3 Schoolmaster spy 1958
4 Contraband Castle 1960

Burkett, Molly

1 Foxes, owls and all 1977
2 A place for animals 1979
Autobiographical series – non-fiction.

Burman, Ben Lucien

1 High water at Catfish Bend 1962
2 Seven stars for Catfish Bend 1962
3 The owl hoots twice at Catfish bend 1967
4 Blow a wild bugle for Catfish Bend 1975
5 High treason at Catfish Bend 1978
1-3 were published in an omnibus edition, 1967. Republished in 2 vols. 1975.

Burnap, Jennifer

THE CARTWRIGHT FAMILY:

1 Journey to Jamestown 1973
2 Beyond the Blue Ridge 1974

Burnett, Frances Eliza Hodgson

1 Sara Crewe: or, what happened at Miss Minchin's 1887
2 Edith's burglar and Sara Crewe 1888
3 A little princess, being the whole story of Sara Crewe now told for the first time 1905

Burningham, John
1 Mr Gumpy's outing 1971
2 Mr Gumpy's motor car 1973
□
1 Come away from the water, Shirley 1977
2 Time to get out of the bath, Shirley 1978

Burton, Hester
1 The rebel 1971
2 Riders of the storm 1972

Butterworth, Ben
1 Trog 1973
2 Trog in trouble 1973
3 Trog tries again 1973
4 Trog's grandpa 1973
5 Trog and his axe 1976
6 Trog and his boat 1976
7 Trog and his dog 1976
8 Trog and his fire 1976
9 Trog makes a trap 1976

Butterworth, Nick
UPNEY JUNCTION:
1 Invasion at Upney Junction
2 Monster at Upney Junction
3 Treasure at Upney Junction
4 A windy day at Upney Junction

Byers, Irene
PENNY AND GILLIAN SERIES:
1 Adventure at Fairborough's Farm 1955
2 Adventure at Dillingdon Dene 1956
3 Adventure at the Blue Cockatoo 1958
TONY AND MELISSA SERIES:
1 Jewel of the jungle 1957
2 Flowers for Melissa 1958
3 Kennel maid Sally 1960
JEREMY AND FENELLA:
1 The strange story of Pippin Wood 1956
2 The missing masterpiece 1957
□
1 Tim of Tamberly Forest 1961
2 Tim returns to Tamberly 1962
3 Trouble at Tamberly 1964
□
1 The stage under the Cedars 1970
2 Camera on Carolyn 1971
□
1 Foresters of Fourways 1963
2 Foresters afield 1966
□
1 The Merediths of Mappins 1964
2 The house of the speckled browns 1967
□
1 Timothy and Tiptoes 1975
2 Tiptoes wins through 1976
3 Tiptoes and the big race 1979

Calveley, Grange
1 When Roobarb didn't find treasure 1975
2 When Roobarb wasn't as pleased as Punch 1975

Cameron, Eleanor
TYCO BASS SERIES:
1 The wonderful flight to the mushroom planet 1954
2 Stowaway to the mushroom planet 1956
3 Mr Bass's planetoid 1958
4 A mystery for Mr Bass 1960
5 Time and Mr Bass 1967

Campbell, Peter
1 The Koalas' spring clean 1972
2 The Koalas' party 1972
3 Amazing Koalas 1978

Cannan, Joanna
1 A pony for Jean 1970
2 Another pony for Jean 1973
3 More ponies for Jean 1976
Partly rewritten by the author's daughter Josephine Pullein-Thompson.

Capon, Paul
1 Warrior's moon 1960
2 The kingdom of the bulls 1961
3 Lord of the chariots 1962
4 The golden cloak 1963

Carey, N. V. *see* **Hitchcock, Alfred** Three Investigators series.

Carlson, Natalie Savage
1 The happy orphelines 1960
2 A brother for the orphelines 1961
3 A pet for the orphelines 1963
4 The orphelines in the enchanted castle 1965
Stories about a French orphanage.

Carpenter, Richard
1 Catweazle 1970
2 Catweazle and the magic zodiac 1971

Carrick, Carol
1 Sleep out 1974
2 Lost in the storm 1976

Carroll, Lewis, *pseud.* **[Charles L. Dodgson]**
1 Alice's adventures in Wonderland 1865
2 Through the looking glass and what Alice found there 1871
□
1 Sylvie and Bruno 1889
2 Sylvie and Bruno, concluded 1893

Carruth, Jane
1 Sally and her puppy 1963
2 Sally on holiday 1963
3 Sally on the farm 1963

Carson, Hilda
1 Plain Mary Jane 1957
2 Mary Jane and the visitors 1959

Carter, Bruce
1 Perilous descent into a strange lost world 1952
2 Speed six! 1953

Case, Patricia
1 Tiger! Tiger! 1949
2 Sons of the tiger 1952

Casement, Christina
1 Wandering Robinson 1970
2 Ringing Robinson 1971
3 Robinson and Slyboots 1974

Cass, Joan
1 Milly Mouse 1975
2 Milly Mouse's measles 1976
□
1 The cat thief 1960
2 The cat show 1962
3 The cats go to market 1969
4 Cats' adventures with car thieves 1980
MOLLY MILLIKINS SERIES:
1 The witch of Witchery Wood 1973
2 The witch and the naughty princesses 1976
3 The witches' lost spell book 1980

Casserley, Anne
1 About Barney 1959
2 Barney the donkey 1960

Cate, Dick
1 Flying free 1975
2 A funny sort of Christmas 1976
3 Old dog, new tricks? 1978
4 A nice day out? 1979

Catherall, Arthur
S.S. BULLDOG SERIES:
1 Ten fathoms deep 1954
2 Jackals of the sea 1955
3 Forgotten submarine 1956
4 Java sea duel 1957
5 Sea wolves 1959
6 Dangerous cargo 1960
7 China Sea jigsaw 1961
8 Prisoners under the sea 1963
9 The strange invader 1964
10 Tanker trap 1965
11 Death of an oil rig 1967
12 Island of forgotten men 1968
13 Red sea rescue 1969
14 Unwilling smuggler 1970
15 Barracuda mystery 1971

Caveney, Sylvia *and* **Stern, Sonia**
1 Little Zip's dressing-up book 1977
2 Little Zip's zoo counting book 1977
3 Little Zip's water book 1978
4 Little Zip's night-time book 1981

Cawley, Winifred
1 Down the long stairs 1964
2 Feast of the serpent 1969
JINNY FRIEND:
1 Gran at Coalgate 1974
2 Silver everything *and* many mansions 1976
2 is about the earlier life of the main character in 1.

Cecil, Hugh *and* **Mirabel**
1 The surprise bear 1982
2 Blue bear's race 1982

3 Speedy bear 1982
4 The bear's Christmas 1982

Chadwick, Doris
1 John of the Sirius 1955
2 John of Sydney Cove 1957
3 John and Nanbaree 1962

Chagnoux, Christine
1 Little Hippo 1971
2 Little Hippo at the circus 1972

Chalmers, Mary
1 Throw a kiss, Harry 1958
2 Take a nap, Harry 1964
3 Merry Christmas, Harry 1978

Chance, Stephen *pseud.* **[Philip Turner]**
REV. SEPTIMUS TRELOAR:
1 Septimus and the Danedyke mystery 1971
2 Septimus and the Minister ghost 1972
3 Septimus and the stone of offering 1976
4 Septimus and the spy ring 1979

Chaney, Jill
1 Christopher's dig 1972
2 Christopher's find 1975
□
1 Mottram Park 1973
2 Return to Mottram Park 1974
□
1 Taking the Woffle to Pebblecombe-on-Sea 1974
2 Woffle, R.A. 1976

Chant, Joy
1 Red moon and black mountain 1970
2 Grey mane of morning 1977

Chapman, Elizabeth
1 Marmaduke the lorry 1952
2 Marmaduke and Joe 1954
3 Riding with Marmaduke 1956
4 Adventures with Marmaduke 1956
5 Merry Marmaduke 1957
6 Marmaduke and his friends 1958
7 Marmaduke and the elephant 1959
8 Marmaduke and the lambs 1960
9 Marmaduke goes to France 1962
10 Marmaduke goes to Holland 1963
11 Marmaduke goes to America 1964
12 Marmaduke goes to Italy 1965
13 Marmaduke goes to Switzerland 1976
14 Marmaduke goes to Spain 1978
15 Marmaduke goes to Morocco 1979
16 Marmaduke in Wales 1982

Chapman, Vera
ARTHURIAN TRILOGY:
1 The green knight 1975
2 King Arthur's daughter 1976
3 The King's damsel 1976

Chard, Brigid
1 A hidden journey 1976
2 Shepherd's Crook 1977

Chase, Lesley
JILL GRAHAM SERIES:
1 Jill Graham and the riddle of the dwarf's shadow 1974
2 Jill Graham and the secret of Druid's Wood 1975
3 Jill Graham and the adventure of the man who vanished 1975
4 Jill Graham and the mystery of the haunted priory 1976
5 Jill Graham and the secret of the silent pool 1980

Chatfield, Keith
1 Issi Noho 1974
2 Issi pandemonium 1975
3 Issi's magic tonic 1976

Chauncy, Nan
LORENNY FAMILY:
1 Tiger in the bush 1957
2 Devil's hill 1958
3 The "Roaring 40" 1963
□
1 They found a cave 1949
2 World's End was home 1952
3 A fortune for the brave 1955
4 Half a world away 1962
Tasmanian stories.

Chell, Mary
LITTLE SLIMTAIL BOOKS:
1 Slimtails 1937
2 More Slimtails 1937
3 Merry Slimtails 1938
4 Slimtails' triplets 1943

5 Slimtails' friends 1940
6 Slimtails at home 1956
7 Mrs Slimtails goes shopping 1979
8 Slimtails' new house 1979
9 Slimtails' picnic 1979

Chesher, Kim
1 The fifth quarter 1976
2 The Carnford inheritance 1977
□
1 Cuthbert and the long winter's sleep 1979
2 Cuthbert and the good ship Thingamabob 1981
3 Cuthbert and the night walkers 1982

Chica
1 Celestine decorates her house 1980
2 Celestine goes to market 1980
3 Celestine to the rescue 1980
4 Celestine high in the sky 1980

Childs, Rob
1 Soccer at Sandford 1980
2 Sandford on the run 1981
3 Sandford on tour 1983

Christopher, John *pseud.* **[C. S. Yeud]**
LUKE OF WINCHESTER SERIES:
1 The Prince in waiting 1970
2 Beyond the burning lands 1971
3 The sword of the spirits 1972
TRIPODS TRILOGY:
1 The white mountains 1967
2 The city of gold and lead 1967
3 The pool of fire 1968
□
1 Fireball 1981
2 New found land 1982

Clare, Helen *pseud.* **[Pauline Clare]**
FIVE DOLLS SERIES:
1 Five dolls in a house 1953
2 Five dolls and the monkey 1956
3 Five dolls in the snow 1957
4 Five dolls and their friends 1959
5 Five dolls and the duke 1963
Republished in 1968 in two omnibus editions.

Clark, Leonard
1 Robert Andrew and Tiffy 1965
2 Robert Andrew and the holy family 1965
3 Robert Andrew by the sea 1965
4 Robert Andrew tells a story 1965
5 Robert Andrew and the Red Indian chief 1966
6 Robert Andrew in the country 1966
7 Robert Andrew and Skippy 1966
□
1 Mr Pettigrew's harvest festival 1974
2 Mr Pettigrew's tram 1975
3 Mr Pettigrew and the bell ringers 1976

Clarke, Pauline
1 James the policeman 1957
2 James and the robbers 1959
3 James and the smugglers 1961
4 James and the black van 1963

Cleary, Beverly
1 The mouse and the motorcycle 1974
2 Runaway Ralph 1974
3 Ralph S. Mouse 1982
□
1 Henry Huggins 1950
2 Henry and Beezus 1952
3 Henry and Ribsy 1954
4 Beezus and Ramona 1955
5 Henry and the clubhouse 1962
6 Ramona the pest 1974
7 Ramona the brave 1975
8 Ramona and her father 1978
9 Ramona and her mother 1979
10 Ramona Quimby age 8 1981

Cleaver, Vera and Bill
1 Ellen Grae 1967
2 Lady Ellen Grae 1968
3 Grover 1971

Clewes, Dorothy
THE HADLEY FAMILY SERIES:
1 Adventure of the scarlet daffodil 1952
2 The mystery of the Blue Admiral 1955
3 Adventure on Rainbow Island 1957
4 The Jade green cadillac 1958
5 The lost tower treasure 1960
6 The singing Strongs 1961
7 Operation smuggle 1964

HENRY HARE SERIES:
1 Henry Hare's boxing match 1950
2 Henry Hare's earthquake 1950
3 Henry Hare, painter and decorator 1951
4 Henry Hare and the kidnapping of Selina Squirrel 1951
□
1 The secret 1956
2 The old pony 1959
□
1 Upside-down Willie 1968
2 Special Branch Willie 1969
3 Fire Brigade Willie 1970
PENNY BOOKS:
1 The runaway 1957
2 The happiest day 1958
3 The birthday 1962
CARRIE AND MAXWELL:
1 Missing from home 1975
2 The testing year 1977

Coatsworth, Elizabeth
1 Away goes Sally 1955
2 Five bushel farm 1958
3 The fair American 1970
4 The white horse of Morocco 1973
5 The wonderful day 1973
□
1 Bob Boddan and the good ship "Rover" 1972
2 Bob Boddan and the Seagoing Farm 1972

Cockett, Mary
1 Jan the market boy 1958
2 Seven days with Jan 1960
□
1 Jasper club 1959
2 There for the picking 1966

Cohen, Miriam
1 Best friends 1972
2 Tough Jim 1975
3 Bee, my Valentine 1979
4 When will I read? 1979
5 New teacher 1980
3 and 4 are by Miriam Cohen and Lillian Hoban.

Colbert, Anthony
1 Amanda has a surprise 1971
2 Amanda goes dancing 1972

Cole, Babette
1 Nungu and the hippopotamus 1978
2 Nungu and the elephant 1980
3 Nungu and the crocodile 1982

Cole, Michael *and* Cole, Joanne
1 Kate and Sam go out 1970
2 Kate and Sam's new home 1970
3 Kate and Sam's pet 1971
4 Kate and Sam's tea 1971
□
1 Bod and the cherry tree 1975
2 Bod's dream 1975
3 Bod's apple 1975
4 Bod in the park 1975
5 Bod's present 1975
6 A lot of Bod 1977
7 Bod and the breakfast 1977
8 Bod and the cake 1977
9 Bod and the dog 1977
10 Bod and the grasshopper 1977
11 Bod and the kite 1977
12 Bod on the beach 1977
6 is an omnibus volume of preceding titles.
□
1 Gran gliding 1983
2 Gran's old bones 1983
3 Gran's good news 1983
4 Gran's pets 1983

Cole, Michael *and* Rogers, Alan
1 The flood 1982
2 Gerald kicks off 1982
3 Light in the sky 1982
4 Pigeon at sea 1982

Coleman, Leslie
1 Wilberforce the whale 1973
2 Wilberforce and the blue cave 1974
3 Wilberforce detective 1975
4 Fort Wilberforce 1977
5 Wilberforce and the McMonster 1978

Collin, Paul Ries
1 Parcel for Henry 1970
2 Up Pepper Lane, down Goose Alley 1971

Collins, Freda
THE WOODLAND PACK:
1 The pack that ran itself 1955

2 The woodland pack 1957
3 The Brownie year 1957
4 Barney and the big house pack 1960
5 The brownies and the Fam-Pig 1964
6 The good turn hunters 1963
7 The pack mascot 1966
8 Patchwork pack 1968

Cookson, Catherine
1 Matty Doolin 1965
2 Joe and the gladiator 1968

Coolidge, Susan
1 What Katy did 1872
2 What Katy did at school 1873
3 What Katy did next 1886
4 Clover 1888
5 In the high valley 1891

Coombs, Patricia
1 Dorrie and the wizard's spell 1968
2 Dorrie and the birthday eggs 1973
3 Dorrie and the haunted house 1973
4 Dorrie and the goblin 1974
5 Dorrie and the blue witch 1975
6 Dorrie and the fortune teller 1975
7 Dorrie and the witch doctor 1977
8 Dorrie's play 1977
9 Dorrie and the witch's imp 1977
10 Dorrie and the amazing elixir 1977
11 Dorrie's magic 1977
12 Dorrie and the weather-box 1977
13 Dorrie and the halloween plot 1978
14 Dorrie and the dreamyard monsters 1979
15 Dorrie and the Screebit ghost 1981

Cooper, Gordon
KATE BASSETT:
1 An hour in the morning 1972
2 A time in a city 1972
3 A certain courage 1975

Cooper, Jilly
1 Little Mabel 1980
2 Little Mabel's great escape 1981
3 Little Mabel wins 1982

Cooper, Michael
1 Meet the Pebbles 1974
2 The Pebbles go to town 1975
3 The Pebbles in the country 1975
4 The Pebbles' night adventure 1976
5 The Pebbles go to sea 1976

Cooper, Susan
THE DARK IS RISING:
1 Over sea, under stone 1965
2 The dark is rising 1973
3 Greenwitch 1974
4 The grey king 1975
5 Silver on the tree 1977

Cope, Kenneth
1 Striker 1976
2 Striker second leg 1977

Cordell, Alexander
JOHN REGAN SERIES:
1 The white cockade 1970
2 Witches' sabbath 1970
3 The healing blade 1971
Trilogy based on the Irish rebellion of 1798.

Coren, Alan
1 The lone Arthur 1976
2 Buffalo Arthur 1976
3 Arthur the kid 1976
4 Arthur's last stand 1977
5 Railroad Arthur 1977
6 Klondike Arthur 1977
7 Arthur and the bellybutton diamond 1979
8 Arthur and the great detective 1979
9 Arthur and the purple panic 1981
10 Arthur versus the rest 1981

Corlett, William
1 The gate of Eden 1974
2 The land beyond 1975
3 Return to the gate 1975

Corson, Hazel Wyman
1 Peter and the moon trip 1962
2 Peter and the rocket ship 1962
3 Peter and the two hour moon 1962
4 Peter and the unlucky rocket 1963
5 Peter and the big balloon 1963

Cosgrove, Brian *and* Hall, M.
1 Sally and Jake and a tortoise 1974
2 Sally and Jake go to the fair 1974

3 Sally and Jake on the farm 1974
4 Sally and Jake play bowls 1974

Craig, George
1 Sir Oliver Bubb and the red knight 1978
2 Sir Oliver Bubb and the wolf 1979

Craig, Karl
1 Emanuel and his parrot 1970
2 Emanuel goes to market 1971

Creche, Sylvia
1 Mervyn the Mouse 1980
2 Hooray for Mervyn Mouse 1982
3 Mervyn Mouse at the zoo 1982
4 Mervyn Mouse joins the sports club 1982
5 Mervyn Mouse at the fair 1982
6 Mervyn Mouse goes camping 1982
2 is an omnibus edition containing four Mervyn Mouse stories.

Cresswell, Helen
1 Jumbo Spencer 1963
2 Jumbo back to nature 1965
3 Jumbo afloat 1966
4 Jumbo and the big dig 1968
□
1 Lizzie Dripping 1973
2 Lizzie Dripping by the sea 1974
3 Lizzie Dripping and the little angel 1974
4 More Lizzie Dripping 1974
'Lizzie Dripping again', 1974 is an omnibus of 2 and 3.
□
1 Two Hoots 1974
2 Two Hoots and the big bad bird 1975
3 Two Hoots in the snow 1975
4 Two Hoots go to the sea 1974
5 Two Hoots play hide and seek 1977
6 Two Hoots and the king 1977
THE BAGTHORPE SAGA:
1 Ordinary Jack 1977
2 Absolute zero 1978
3 Bagthorpes unlimited 1978
4 Bagthorpes versus the world 1979
□
1 My aunt Polly 1979
2 My aunt Polly by the sea 1980

Crompton, Richmal *pseud.* **[Richmal Crompton Lamburn]**
1 Just William 1922
2 More William 1923
3 William again 1923
4 William the fourth 1924
5 Still William 1925
6 William the Conqueror 1926
7 William in trouble 1927
8 William the outlaw 1927
9 William the good 1928
10 William 1929
11 William the bad 1930
12 William's happy days 1930
13 William's crowded hours 1931
14 William the pirate 1932
15 William the rebel 1933
16 William the gangster 1934
17 William the detective 1935
18 Sweet William 1936
19 William the showman 1937
20 William the dictator 1938
21 William and the A.R.P. 1939
22 William and the evacuees 1940
23 William carries on 1942
24 William does his bit 1941
25 William and the Brains Trust 1945
26 Just William's luck 1948
27 William the bold 1950
28 William and the tramp 1952
29 William and the moon rocket 1954
30 William and the space animal 1956
31 William the explorer 1960
32 William's television show 1958
33 William's treasure trove 1962
34 William and the witch 1964
35 William and the pop singers 1965
36 William and the masked ranger 1966
37 William the superman 1968
38 William the lawless 1970
39 William the hero 1974
21 republished as 'William the film star' 1956. 22 republished as 'William's bad resolution' 1956.
JIMMY SERIES:
1 Jimmy 1949
2 Jimmy again 1951
3 Jimmy the third 1951

Cross, Gillian
1 Save our school 1981
2 The Mintyglo kid 1982

Cross, J. K.
1 Angry planet 1945
2 SOS from Mars 1954

Crossley-Holland, Kevin *see* **Holland, Kevin Crossley**

Cunliffe, John
1 Farmer Barnes buys a pig 1964
2 Farmer Barnes and Bluebell 1966
3 Farmer Barnes at the county show 1969
4 Farmer Barnes and the goats 1971
5 Farmer Barnes goes fishing 1972
6 Farmer Barnes and the snow picnic 1974
7 Farmer Barnes and the harvest doll 1977
8 Farmer Barnes fells a tree 1977
9 Farmer Barnes Guy Fawkes' day 1978
POSTMAN PAT SERIES:
1 Postman Pat and the mystery thief 1981
2 Postman Pat's treasure hunt 1981
3 Postman Pat's rainy day 1982
4 Postman Pat's secret 1982
5 Postman Pat's difficult day 1982
6 Postman Pat's foggy day 1982
7 Postman Pat's tractor express 1983
8 Postman Pat takes a message 1983
MR GOSLING STORIES:
1 Mr Gosling and the runaway chair 1978
2 Mr Gosling and the great art robbery 1979

Curry, Jane Louise
1 The house napper 1971
2 The lost farm 1974
The fantastic events of 2 occur within the story of 1.
ABALOC STORIES:
1 Beneath the hill 1968
2 The daybreakers 1970
3 Over the sea's edge 1971
4 The watchers 1976
5 The birdstones 1978

Curtis, Philip
1 Mr Browser and the brain sharpeners 1979
2 Mr Browser meets the Burrowers 1980
3 Mr Browser and the comet crisis 1981
4 The revenge of the brain sharpeners 1982
5 Mr Browser and the mini-meteorites 1983
6 Beware of the brain sharpeners 1983

Dahl, Roald
1 Charlie and the chocolate factory 1964
2 Charlie and the great glass elevator 1973
The above can also be found in one volume, 'Complete adventures of Charlie and Mr Willie Wonka' 1978.

Dahlerup, Rina
BUFFY AND CO:
1 Buffy cleans up 1979
2 Friends again 1979

Dale, Judith
1 Shirley Flight – air hostess 1958
2 Shirley Flight – air hostess – and the diamond smugglers 1958
3 Shirley Flight – air hostess – desert adventure 1958
4 Shirley Flight – air hostess – in Hollywood 1959
5 Shirley Flight – air hostess – and the Flying Doctor 1959
6 Shirley Flight – air hostess – and the rajah's daughter 1959
7 Shirley Flight – air hostess – in Congo rescue 1960
8 Shirley Flight and the great bullion mystery 1960
9 Shirley Flight – air hostess – the fjord adventure 1961
10 Shirley Flight – air hostess – and the Pacific castaways 1961
11 Shirley Flight – air hostess – and the Chinese Puzzle 1962
12 Shirley Flight – air hostess – flying jet 1962
13 Shirley Flight – air hostess – Canadian capers 1962
14 Shirley Flight – air hostess – in storm warning 1963
15 Shirley Flight in Hawaiian mystery 1963
16 Shirley Flight in Spain 1963

Dallas, Ruth
1 The children in the bush 1969
2 The wild boy in the bush 1971
3 The big flood in the bush 1972

Dann, Colin
1 The animals of Farthing Wood 1979
2 In the grip of winter 1981
3 Fox's feud 1982
4 Fox Cub bold 1983

Darke, Marjorie
FRANCES REDMAYNE SERIES:
1 Ride the iron horse 1973
2 The star trap 1974
□
1 Kipper's return 1976
2 Kipper skips 1979

Dauer, Rosamond
1 Bullfrog builds a house 1979
2 Bullfrog grows up

Davies, Andrew
1 Marmalade and Rufus 1979
2 Marmalade Atkins in space 1982
3 Educating Marmalade 1983
1 reprinted as 'Marmalade Atkins' dreadful deeds' 1982.

Davies, Evelyn
1 Little Bear the brave 1976
2 Little Bear's feather, and run for home 1976
3 Little Bear's journey 1979
4 The little foxes 1977

Davies, Hunter
1 Flossy Teacake's fur coat 1982
2 Flossy Teacake again 1983

Davis, Gerry *see* **Dr Who series**

Dawlish, Peter *pseud.* **[James Lennox Kerr]**
PEG-LEG SERIES:
1 Peg-Leg and the fur pirates 1939
2 Captain Peg-Leg's war 1939
3 Peg-Leg and the invaders 1940
4 Peg-Leg sweeps the sea 1940
DAUNTLESS SERIES:
1 Dauntless finds her crew 1947
2 Dauntless sails again 1948
3 Dauntless and the 'Mary Baines' 1949
4 Dauntless takes recruits 1950
5 Dauntless sails in 1952
6 Dauntless in danger 1954
7 Dauntless goes home 1960

Dawson, Alec John
1 Finn the wolfhound 1908
2 Jan, son of Finn 1917

Dawson, Helen
NOREEN AND AUNTY JOAN:
1 Noreen's first case 1959
2 The house in Haven Street 1960
3 Noreen and the Barclay affair 1963
4 Noreen and the missing schoolgirl 1963
5 Noreen and the Henry affair 1965
6 Noreen and the mystery hero 1965

Deary, Terry
1 The custard kid 1978
2 Calamity Kate 1980

De Brunhoff, Jean
1 The story of Babar 1933
2 Babar's travels 1934
3 Babar the king 1936
4 Babar's friend Zephir 1937
5 Babar at home 1938
6 Babar and Father Christmas 1940
7 Babar and that rascal Arthur 1948
8 Picnic at Babar's 1950
9 Babar's visit to Bird Island 1952
10 Babar's fair 1954
11 Babar and the professor 1954
12 Babar goes to America 1956
13 Babar's castle 1962
14 Babar's birthday surprise 1971
15 Babar on the secret planet
7-13 are by L. de Brunhoff. 15 was published in 1974 as 'Babar visits another planet'.
LITTLE BABAR BOOKS:
1 Babar's childhood
2 Babar and the old lady
3 Babar's coronation
4 Babar's balloon trip
5 Babar at the circus
6 Babar goes skiing
7 Babar's kingdom
8 Long live King Babar
9 Babar and his children
10 Babar and the crocodile
11 Babar the gardener
12 Babar at the seaside
13 Babar in the snow
14 Babar's day out
15 Babar and the doctor

16 Babar and the Christmas tree
17 Babar goes camping
18 Babar the artist
19 Babar the sportsman
20 Babar the cook
21 Babar the pilot
22 Babar the musician
23 Babar goes visiting
24 Babar learns to drive
25 Babar keeps fit
26 Babar and the Wully-Wully 1977
27 Babar's mystery 1979
These are miniature editions with individual episodes from the main series. 'Babar's little story book' 1979 contains 'Babar at the seaside', 'Babar the gardener', 'Babar in the snow' and 'Babar and the crocodile. 'Babar's day out and other stories' 1980 contains 'Babar's day out', 'Babar the pilot', 'Babar the sportsman' and 'Babar goes camping'. 'Babar's Anniversary Album: 6 favourite books' 1982 contains three stories from 'Father and Son'.

De Brunhoff, Laurent
1 Serafina the giraffe 1961
2 Serafina's lucky find 1967
3 Captain Serafina 1969

Dehn, Olive
1 Tabby magic 1959
2 More Tabby magic 1960
THE MEREDITH CHILDREN:
1 The caretakers 1960
2 The caretakers and the poacher 1961
3 The caretakers and the gypsy 1962
4 The caretakers to the rescue 1964
5 Caretakers of Wilmhurst 1966

De Larrabeit, Michael
1 The Borribles 1976
2 The Borribles go for broke 1981

Delgado, Alan
MIKE AND CAROLINE:
1 The very hot water-bottle 1962
2 Hide the slipper 1963

Del Rey, Lester
1 Outpost of Jupiter 1966
2 The runaway robot 1967

Denes, G.
JOHN AND JENNIFER:
1 Jennifer goes to school 1945
2 John and Jennifer at the zoo 1946
3 Christmas at Timothy's 1947
4 John and Jennifer at the farm 1948
5 John and Jennifer at the circus 1949
6 John and Jennifer and their pets
7 John and Jennifer's treasure hunt 1953
8 John and Jennifer go camping 1954
9 John and Jennifer's pony club
10 John and Jennifer go to London 1956
11 John and Jennifer go sailing 1957
12 John and Jennifer's concert party 1957
13 John and Jennifer go travelling 1957
14 John and Jennifer at London airport 1958

"Derib" and "Job"
1 Yakari 1978
2 Yakari and the white buffalo 1979
Cartoon storybooks, the adventures of a little Indian brave.

Derwent, Lavinia
1 Macpherson 1961
2 Macpherson's funnybone 1962
3 Macpherson's highland fling 1963
4 Macpherson in Edinburgh 1964
5 Macpherson in America 1965
6 Macpherson sails the seas 1966
7 Macpherson on the farm 1967
8 Macpherson's caravan 1968
9 Macpherson's skyscraper 1969
10 Macpherson's island 1970
11 Macpherson's mystery adventure 1982
12 Macpherson's winter sports
MAGNUS SERIES:
1 Sula 1971
2 Return to Sula 1972
3 The boy from Sula 1973
4 Song of Sula 1976

Dickens, Frank
1 Boffo, the great motor-cycle race 1976
2 Boffo, the great air race 1976
□
1 Albert Herbert Hawkins, the naughtiest boy in the world 1978

2 Albert Herbert Hawkins and the space rocket 1978
3 Albert Herbert Hawkins and the Olympic Games 1980

Dickens, Monica
1 Cobblers dream 1963
2 Follyfoot 1971
3 Dora at Follyfoot 1972
4 The horses of Follyfoot 1975
5 Strangers at Follyfoot 1976
'Follyfoot Farm' 1973 is an omnibus volume of 2 and 3.
THE FIELDING FAMILY:
1 The house at World's End 1970
2 Summer at World's End 1971
3 World's End in Winter 1972
4 Spring comes to World's End 1973

Dickinson, Mary
1 Alex's bed 1980
2 Alex and Roy 1981
3 Alex's outing 1983

Dickinson, Peter
THE CHANGES:
1 The weathermonger 1968
2 Heartease 1969
3 The devil's children 1970
Published in one volume under the title 'The Changes', a trilogy 1975.

Dicks, Terrance
THE BAKER STREET IRREGULARS:
1 The Baker Street Irregulars: the case of the missing masterpiece 1978
2 The Baker Street Irregulars: the case of the Fagin File 1978
3 The Baker Street Irregulars: the case of the Blackmail Boys 1979
4 The Baker Street Irregulars: the case of the cinema swindle 1980
5 The Baker Street Irregulars: the case of the ghost grabbers 1980
6 The Baker Street Irregulars: the case of the cop catchers 1981
□
1 Star quest: spacejack 1978
2 Star quest: Roboworld 1979
3 Star quest: Terrosaur 1981
□
1 Ask Oliver: The mystery of the missing diamond 1982
2 Ask Oliver: The mystery of the haunted hospital 1982
3 Ask Oliver: The mystery of the smugglers' treasure 1983
'HORROR' SERIES:
1 Cry vampire! 1981
2 Marvin's monster 1982
3 Wereboy . . . ! 1982
4 Demon of the dark 1983
5 War of the witches 1983

Dicks, T. *see also* **Dr Who series**

Digby, Anne
1 First term at Trebizon 1978
2 Second term at Trebizon 1979
3 Summer term at Trebizon 1979
4 Boy trouble at Trebizon 1980
5 More trouble at Trebizon 1981
6 Tennis term at Trebizon 1982
7 Summer camp at Trebizon 1982
8 Into the fourth at Trebizon 1982

Dixon, Franklin W.
THE HARDY BOYS SERIES:
1 The secret of the tunnel 1969
2 Sign of the crooked arrow
3 Phantom freighter
4 House on the cliff
5 Tower treasure
6 Secret of the old mill
7 Missing chums
8 Hunting for hidden gold
9 Shore Road mystery
10 Secret of the caves
11 Mystery of Cabin Island
12 Great airport mystery
13 Secret of Skull Mountain 1966
14 The secret panel 1967
15 What happened at midnight
16 While the clock ticked
17 Footprints under the window
18 Mark on the door
19 Hidden harbour mystery
20 The sinister signpost 1969
21 A figure in hiding 1968
22 The secret warning 1968

23 The twisted claw 1968
24 The disappearing floor 1961
25 The mystery of the flying express 1961
26 The clue of the broken blade 1963
27 The flickering torch mystery 1963
28 The melted coins 1967
29 The short-wave mystery 1967
30 The wailing siren mystery 1966
31 Secret of the wild cat swamp 1966
32 Pursuit patrol
33 Mystery of the desert giant 1963
34 The clue of the screeching owl 1969
35 The secret of Pirate's hill 1965
36 The ghost at Skeleton Rock 1964
37 The Viking symbol mystery 1964
38 The mystery of the Aztec warrior 1964
39 The mystery at Devil's Paw 1963
40 The mystery of the Chinese junk 1963
41 The crisscross shadow 1965
42 The yellow feather mystery 1965
43 The hooded hawk mystery 1965
44 The clue in the embers 1965
45 The mystery of the spiral ridge 1967
46 The haunted fort 1966
47 Arctic patrol mystery
48 Mystery of the tattoo
49 The secret agent on Flight 101 1969
50 The mysterious caravan 1977
51 Danger on Vampire Trail 1977
52 The sting of the scorpion
53 The witchmaster's key
54 The Bombay boomerang
55 The clue of the hissing serpent
56 The firebird rocket
57 The jungle pyramid
58 Masked monkey
59 The shattered helmet
60 Mystery of the Samurai sword
61 Night of the werewolf
62 The apeman's secret
63 The Pentagon spy
64 The stone idol
65 The vanishing thieves
66 The outlaw's silver
67 The submarine caper
68 The mummy case 1981
69 Mystery of smuggler's cove 1981
70 Four headed dragon

'The Hardy Boys detective handbook' 1979 and 'Super sleuths'—stories featuring Hardy Boys and Nancy Drew 1983.

Dixon, Rex, *pseud.* **[Reginald Alec Martin]**

POCOMOTO SERIES:

1 Pocomoto, pony express rider 1955
2 Pocomoto, tenderfoot 1955
3 Pocomoto and the canyon treasure 1954
4 Pocomoto and the night riders 1953
5 Pocomoto, Bronco buster 1953
6 Pocomoto, brush popper 1954
7 Pocomoto and the l'il fella 1954
8 Pocomoto, buffalo hunter 1954
9 Pocomoto—cowboy cavalier 1959
10 Pocomoto and the lazy river 1955
11 Pocomoto and the snow wolf 1955
12 Pocomoto and the Indian trails 1956
13 Pocomoto and the Sierra pioneers
14 Pocomoto and the Spanish steed 1957
15 Pocomoto and the golden herd 1960
16 Pocomoto and the robbers' trail 1956
17 Pocomoto and the desert gold 1957
18 Pocomoto and the circus folk 1957
19 Pocomoto and the warrior braves 1961
20 Pocomoto and the Texas pioneers 1958
21 Pocomoto and the lazy sheriff 1958
22 Pocomoto and the lost hunters 1959
23 Pocomoto and the Texas ranger 1960
24 Pocomoto and the desert braves 1961
25 Pocomoto and the Mexican bandits 1963

Dobson, Julia

CRISP TWINS:

1 The animal rescuers 1982
2 The wreck finders 1982
3 Danger in the magic kingdom 1983

Doctor Who series:

1 Doctor Who 1964
2 Doctor Who and the Zarbi by B. Strutton 1965
3 Doctor Who and the Crusaders by D. Whitaker 1965
4 Doctor Who and the Daleks by D. Whitaker 1973
5 Doctor Who and the cave-monsters by M. Hulke 1974
6 Doctor Who and the Auton invasion by M. Hulke 1974
7 Doctor Who and the abominable snowmen by T. Dicks 1974
8 Doctor Who and the sea devils by M. Hulke 1974
9 Doctor Who and the day of the Daleks by T. Dicks 1974

10 Doctor Who and the doomsday weapon by M. Hulke 1974
11 Doctor Who and the curse of Peladon by B. Hayles 1974
12 Doctor Who and the Cybermen by G. Davis
13 Doctor Who and the tenth planet by G. Davis 1976
14 Doctor Who meets the Loch Ness monster by T. Dicks 1975
15 Doctor Who and the giant robot by T. Dicks 1975
16 Doctor Who and the dinosaur invasion by M. Hulke 1975
17 Doctor Who and the green death by M. Hulke 1975
18 Doctor Who and the daemons by B. Letts 1975
19 Doctor Who: the three doctors by T. Dicks 1975
20 Doctor Who and the ice warriors by B. Hayles 1976
21 Doctor Who and the revenge of the Cybermen by T. Dicks 1976
22 Doctor Who and the planet of spiders by T. Dicks 1976
23 Doctor Who and the genesis of the Daleks by T. Dicks 1976
24 Doctor Who and the web of fear by T. Dicks 1976
25 Doctor Who and the space war by M. Hulke 1976
26 Doctor Who and the planet of the Daleks by T. Dicks 1976
27 Doctor Who and the pyramid of Mars by T. Dicks 1977
28 Doctor Who and the carnival of monsters by T. Dicks 1977
29 Doctor Who and the seeds of doom by P. Hinchcliffe 1977
30 Doctor Who and the Dalek invasion of earth by T. Dicks 1977
31 Doctor Who and the ark in space by I. Marter 1977
32 Doctor Who and the claws of Axos by T. Dicks 1977
33 Doctor Who and the brain of Morbius by T. Dicks 1977
34 Doctor Who and the planet of evil by T. Dicks 1977
35 Doctor Who and the deadly assassin by T. Dicks 1977
36 Doctor Who and the mutants by T. Dicks 1977
37 Doctor Who and the talons of Weng-Chiang by T. Dicks 1977
38 Doctor Who and the face of evil by T. Dicks 1978
39 Doctor Who and the masque of Mandragora by P. Hinchcliffe 1977
40 Doctor Who and the horror of Fang Rock by T. Dicks 1978
41 Doctor Who and the tomb of the Cybermen by G. Davis 1978
42 Doctor Who and the time warrior by T. Dicks 1978
43 Doctor Who death to the Daleks by T. Dicks 1978
44 Doctor Who and the android invasion by T. Dicks 1978
45 Doctor Who and the sontaran experiment by I. Marter 1978
46 Doctor Who and the hand of fear by T. Dicks 1979
47 Doctor Who and the invisible enemy by T. Dicks 1979
48 Doctor Who and the robots of death by T. Dicks 1979
49 Doctor Who and the image of the Fendahl by T. Dicks 1979
50 Doctor Who and the war games by M. Hulke 1979
51 Doctor Who and the destiny of the Daleks by T. Dicks 1979
52 Doctor Who and the ribos operation by I. Maret 1979
53 Doctor Who and the underworld by T. Dicks 1979
54 Doctor Who and the invasion of time by T. Dicks 1980
55 Doctor Who and the androids of Tara by T. Dicks 1980
56 Doctor Who and the stones of blood by T. Dicks 1980
57 Doctor Who and the power of Kroll by T. Dicks 1980
58 Doctor Who and the armageddon factor by T. Dicks 1980
59 Doctor Who and the keys of Marinus by P. Hinchcliffe 1980
60 Doctor Who and the nightmare of Eden by T. Dicks 1980
61 Doctor Who and the horns of Nimon by T. Dicks 1980

62 Doctor Who and the monster of Peladon by T. Dicks 1980
63 Doctor Who and the creature from the pit by D. Fisher 1980
64 Doctor Who and the terror of autons by D. Dicks 1980
65 Doctor Who and the enemy of the world by I. Marter 1980
66 Doctor Who and the state of decay by T. Dicks 1980
67 Doctor Who and the Auton invasion by T. Dicks 1981
68 Doctor Who and an unearthly child by T. Dicks 1981
This is the very first Doctor Who story – only published in 1981.
69 Doctor Who and the Keeper of Traken by T. Dicks 1982
70 Doctor Who and Warrior's gate by J. Lydecker 1982
71 Doctor Who and the leisure hive by D. Fisher 1982
72 Doctor Who – Logopolis by C. H. Bidmead 1982
73 Doctor Who and the sunmakers by T. Dicks 1982
74 Doctor Who and the visitation by E. Saward 1982
75 Doctor Who: Meglos by T. Dicks 1983
76 Doctor Who: Castroralva by C. H. Bidmead 1983
77 Doctor Who: Four to Doomsday by T. Dicks 1983
78 Doctor Who: Timeflight by P. Grimwade 1983

Dodd, Maurice
PERISHERS' SERIES:
1 Boot's book 1979
2 Maisie's book 1979
3 Marlon's book 1979
4 Wellington's book 1979

Donaldson, Margaret
1 Journey into war 1979
2 The moon's on fire 1980

Dowling, Patrick
1 The big match and poor old Morph 1981
2 Birthday party 1981
3 Swimming pool 1981

Drake, Joan
MR GRIMPWINKLE SERIES:
1 The jiggle woggle bus 1957
2 Mr Grimpwinkle 1958
3 Mr Grimpwinkle's marrow 1959
4 Mr Grimpwinkle – pirate cook 1960
5 Mr Grimpwinkle buys a house 1960
6 Mr Grimpwinkle buys a bus 1961
7 Mr Grimpwinkle's holiday 1962
8 Mr Grimpwinkle's visitor 1964
□
1 Mr Bubbus and the apple-green engine 1975
2 Mr Bubbus and the railway smugglers 1976
3 Mr Bubbus and the railway rescue 1978

Drew, Patricia
1 Hogglespike 1971
2 Hogglespike and Thistle 1972
3 Hogglespike in danger 1973

Drummond, Violet Hilda
1 Mrs Easter's parasol 1944
2 Mrs Easter and the storks 1957
3 Mrs Easter and the Golden Bounder 1970
4 Mrs Easter's Christmas flight 1972
□
1 Miss Anna Truly 1945
2 Miss Anna Truly and the Christmas lights 1968
□
1 Little Laura's cat 1960
2 Little Laura on the river 1960
3 Little Laura and the lonely ostrich 1963
4 Little Laura and her best friend 1963
5 Little Laura and the thief 1963

Du Bois, William Pene
1 Giant Otto 1937
2 Otto at sea 1937
3 Otto in Texas 1961
4 Otto in Africa 1962
5 Otto and the magic potatoes 1970 (USA)
□
1 The alligator case 1965
2 The horse in the camel suit 1967

Duff, Douglas Valder
1 Bill Berenger's first case 1948
2 Berenger to the rescue 1949

3 Berenger's toughest case 1951
4 Bill Berenger wins command 1950

ADAM MACADAM, NAVAL CADET:

1 Sea serpent island 1956
2 Ocean haul 1956
3 The San Matteo 1957
4 Sea-bed treasure 1957
5 Black ivory 1958
6 Undersea oil tanker 1959
7 At close grips 1959
8 Crusader's gold 1959
9 The king's rescue 1959
10 Pirates aboard 1960
11 The stolen aircraft carrier 1961
12 Red sea blackbirders 1961
13 The pale grey man 1962

JEREMY SERIES:

1 The ship-slayers 1953
2 The miracle man 1953
3 Operation sunpower 1955

□

1 Yarns of a shellback 1959
2 More yarns of a shellback 1960

Dumas, Philippe

1 The story of Edward 1977
2 Lucy, Edward's daughter 1977

□

1 Laura, Alice's new puppy 1979
2 Laura on the road 1979
3 Laura and the bandits 1980
4 Laura loses her head 1981

Duncan, Jane

1 Camerons on the trail 1963
2 Camerons on the hills 1963
3 Camerons at the castle 1964
4 Camerons calling 1966
5 Camerons ahoy! 1968

□

1 Herself and Janet Reachfar 1975
2 Janet Reachfar and the Kelpie 1976
3 Janet Reachfar and the Chickabird 1978
Connected with the adult 'Reachfar' series.

Dunnett, Margaret

THE COBB FAMILY:

1 The people next door 1965
2 Has anyone seen Emmy? 1968
3 The boy who saw Emmy 1973

Du Soe, Robert

PEDRO, THE FISHERMAN:

1 Three without fear 1947
2 Sea boots 1949

Duvoisin, Roger

1 Veronica 1962
2 Veronica goes to Petunia's farm 1963
3 Lonely Veronica 1964
4 Veronica's smile 1965
5 Veronica and the birthday present 1972

□

1 Petunia 1958
2 Petunia and the song 1951 (USA)
3 Petunia's Christmas 1960
4 Petunia takes a trip 1959
5 Petunia, beware! 1962
6 Petunia I love you 1966
7 Petunia's treasure 1977

□

1 Crocodile in the tree 1972
2 Crocus 1977
3 The importance of crocus 1977

Dyer, Elinor M. Brent-

CHALET SCHOOL SERIES:

1 The school at the Chalet 1925
2 Jo of the Chalet School 1926
3 The princess of the Chalet School 1927
4 The head-girl of the Chalet School 1928
5 The rivals at the Chalet School 1929
6 Eustacia goes to the Chalet School 1930
7 The Chalet School and Jo 1931
8 The Chalet girls in camp 1932
9 The exploits of the Chalet girls 1933
10 The Chalet School and the Lintons 1934
11 The new house at the Chalet School 1935
12 Jo returns to the Chalet School 1936
13 The new Chalet School 1938
14 The Chalet School in exile 1940
15 The Chalet School goes to it 1941
16 The Highland twins at the Chalet School 1942
17 Lavender laughs in the Chalet School 1943
18 Gay from China at the Chalet School 1944
19 Jo to the rescue 1945
20 Three go to the Chalet School 1949
21 The Chalet School and the Island 1950
22 Peggy of the Chalet School 1950

23 Chalet School and Rosalie 1951
24 Carola storms the Chalet School 1951
25 The wrong Chalet School 1952
26 Shocks for the Chalet School 1952
27 The Chalet School in the Oberland 1952
28 Bride leads the Chalet School 1953
29 Changes for the Chalet School 1953
30 Joey goes to the Oberland 1954
31 The Chalet School and Barbara 1954
32 Tom tackles the Chalet School 1955
33 The Chalet School does it again 1955
34 A Chalet girl from Kenya 1955
35 Mary Lou of the Chalet School 1956
36 A genius at the Chalet School 1956
37 A problem at the Chalet School 1956
38 The new mistress at the Chalet School 1957
39 Excitements at the Chalet School 1957
40 The coming of age of the Chalet School 1958
41 The Chalet School and Richenda 1958
42 Trials for the Chalet School 1959
43 Theodora and the Chalet School 1959
44 Joey and Co. in Tirol 1960
45 Ruey Richardson – Chaletian 1960
46 A leader in the Chalet School 1961
47 The Chalet School wins the trick 1961
48 A future Chalet School girl 1962
49 The feud in the Chalet School 1962
50 The Chalet School triplets 1963
51 The Chalet School reunion 1963
52 Jane and the Chalet School 1964
53 Redheads at the Chalet School 1964
54 Adrienne and the Chalet School 1965
55 Summer term at the Chalet School 1965
56 Challenge for the Chalet School 1966
57 Two Sams at the Chalet School 1967
58 Althea joins the Chalet School 1969
59 Prefects of the Chalet School 1970

23 was published only in paperback and did not form part of the hardback series. Sequentially it precedes 21. 33 was first published in 1948/49 as 'The first Chalet book for girls' and 'The second Chalet book for girls'. Sequentially it follows number 20.

LA ROCHELLE SERIES:

1 Gerry goes to school 1922
2 A head girl's difficulties 1923
3 The maids of La Rochelle 1924
4 Seven scamps 1927
5 Heather leaves school 1929
6 Janie of La Rochelle 1932
7 Janie steps in 1953

□

1 Lorna at Wynyards 1947
2 Stepsister for Lorna 1948

□

1 The school at Skelton Hall 1962
2 Trouble at Skelton Hall 1963

CHUDLEIGH HOLD SERIES:

1 Chudleigh Hold 1954
2 The Condor Crags adventure 1954
3 Top secret 1955

□

1 Fardingales 1950
2 The 'Susannah' adventure 1953

'Caroline the second' 1937 is about the same school as 'A thrilling term at Janeways' 1927 and a character in the story is descended from the heroine of 'Elizabeth the gallant' 1935. Details from Helen McClelland's 'Behind the Chalet School' 1981.

Dyke, John

1 Pigwig and the pirates 1979
2 Pigwig and the crusty diamonds 1982

Eadington, Joan

1 Jonny Briggs 1977
2 Jonny Briggs and the Ghost 1978
3 Jonny Briggs and the Whitby weekend 1979
4 Jonny Briggs and the great razzle dazzle 1981
5 Jonny Briggs and the giant cave 1982
6 Jonny Briggs and the galloping wedding 1983

'The adventures of Jonny Briggs' 1979 is an omnibus volume containing 1, 2, 3 and 4.

Eagar, Edward

1 Half magic 1954
2 Knight's castle 1956
3 Magic by the lake 1957
4 The time garden 1959
5 Magic or not? 1959
6 The well-wishers 1961
7 Seven-day magic 1963

Eagar, Frances

LAURA AND HARRY SERIES:

1 The little sparrow 1971
2 The tin mine 1972
3 Midnight patrol 1974

Earnshaw, Brian

1 Dragonfall 5 and the royal beast 1972
2 Dragonfall 5 and the space cowboys 1972
3 Dragonfall 5 and the empty planet 1973
4 Dragonfall 5 and the hijackers 1974
5 Dragonfall 5 and the master mind 1975
6 Dragonfall 5 and the super horse 1977
7 Dragonfall 5 and the haunted world 1979

Ecke, Wolfgang

SUPER SLEUTH SERIES:

1 The case of the face at the window 1973
2 The case of the stolen paintings 1979
3 The case of the invisible witness 1980
4 The case of the bank hold-up 1982

Edgar, Marriott

1 Lion and Albert 1980
2 Albert comes back 1980

Illustrated versions of the Stanley Holloway monologues.

Edwards, David

1 The Appleyards 1955
2 The Appleyards again 1956

Edwards, Dorothy

1 My naughty little sister 1952
2 More naughty little sister stories 1957
3 My naughty little sister's friends 1968
4 When my naughty little sister was good 1968
5 My naughty little sister and Bad Harry 1974

'My naughty little sister goes fishing' 1976, 'My naughty little sister and Bad Harry's rabbit' 1977, and 'My naughty little sister at the fair' 1979 are published in the 'New look book series' format aimed at younger children.

□

1 Tales of Joe and Timothy 1969
2 Joe and Timothy together 1971

Edwards, Hugh

SEA WITCH SERIES:

1 Tiger shark 1976
2 Sea Lion Island 1977
3 The pearl pirates 1978
4 The crocodile god 1982

Edwards, Lynne *and* Edwards, Brian

1 Dead as a dodo 1973
2 The dodo is a solitary bird 1977
3 Mad Dan dodo in outer space 1979

Edwards, Monica

PUNCHBOWL FARM SERIES:

1 No mistaking Corker 1947
2 Black hunting whip 1950
3 Punchbowl midnight 1951
4 Spirit of Punchbowl farm 1952
5 The wanderer 1953
6 Punchbowl harvest 1954
7 Frenchman's secret 1956
8 The cownappers 1958
9 The outsider 1961
10 Fire in the punchbowl 1965
11 The wild one 1967

9 and 10 include characters from Romney Marsh series.

ROMNEY MARSH SERIES:

1 Wish for a pony 1947
2 Summer of the great secret 1948
3 The midnight horse 1949
4 The white riders 1950
5 Cargo of horses 1951
6 Hidden in a dream 1952
7 Storm ahead 1953
8 No entry 1954
9 The nightbird 1955
10 Operation seabird 1957
11 Strangers to the Marsh 1957
12 No going back 1960
13 The hoodwinkers 1962
14 Killer dog 1962
15 Dolphin summer 1959
16 A wind is blowing 1969

Edwards, Sylvia

SALLY BAXTER GIRL REPORTER SERIES:

1 Sally Baxter – girl reporter – in Canada 1958
2 Sally Baxter – girl reporter – and the mystery heiress 1958

3 Sally Baxter – girl reporter – and the runaway princess 1958
4 Sally Baxter – girl reporter – on location 1958
5 African alibi 1959
6 Sally Baxter – girl reporter – the family holiday 1959
7 Sally Baxter – girl reporter – in Australia 1959
8 Sally Baxter – girl reporter – and the underwater adventure 1959
9 The golden yacht 1961
10 Secret island 1961
11 The Shamrock mystery 1961
12 Strangers in Fleet Street

Elliot, Janice
1 The birthday unicorn 1971
2 Alexander in the land of Mog 1973

Elliot, Margaret
1 When the night crow flies 1977
2 Witch's gold 1979
3 To trick a witch 1981

Ellison, Norman Frederick
1 Wandering with Nomad 1946
2 Out of doors with Nomad 1947
3 Over the hills with Nomad 1948
4 Roving with Nomad 1949
5 Adventuring with Nomad 1950
6 Northwards with Nomad 1951

Engdahl, Sylvia
1 Enchantress from the stars 1974
2 The far side of evil 1975

Enright, Dennis Joseph
1 The joke shop 1976
2 Wild ghost chase 1978
3 Beyond Land's End 1979

Enright, Elizabeth, ***pseud.*** **[Elizabeth Wright Enright Gillham]**
THE MELENDY FAMILY SERIES:
1 The Saturdays 1955
2 The four-storey mistake 1955
3 Then there were five 1956
4 Spiderweb for two 1956

PORTIA AND JULIAN:
1 Gone-away lake 1957
2 Return to Gone-away 1962

Erickson, Russell
WARTON AND MORTON SERIES:
1 A toad for Tuesday 1979
2 Warton and Morton 1979
3 Warton's Christmas Eve adventure 1979
4 Warton and the king of the skies 1980
5 Warton and the traders 1981
6 Warton and the castaways 1982

Estes, Eleanor
1 The Moffats 1941
2 The middle Moffat 1942
3 Rufus M 1943
□
1 Pinky Pye 1959
2 Ginger Pye 1961

Estoril, Jean
1 Ballet for Drina 1957
2 Drina's dancing year 1958
3 Drina dances in exile 1959
4 Drina dances in Italy 1959
5 Drina dances again 1960
6 Drina dances in New York 1961
7 Drina dances in Paris 1962
8 Drina dances in Madeira 1963
9 Drina dances in Switzerland 1964
10 Drina goes on tour 1965

Ets, Marie Hall
1 Mister Penny 1957
2 Mister Penny's race horse 1958
3 Mister Penny's circus 1961 (USA)

Evans, James Roose-
ODD AND ELSEWHERE SERIES:
1 Adventures of Odd and Elsewhere 1971
2 The secret of the seven bright shiners 1972
3 Odd and the Great Bear 1973
4 Elsewhere and the gathering of the clowns 1974
5 The return of the great bear 1975
6 The secret of Tippity Witchet 1975
7 The lost treasure of Wales 1977

Faber, Nancy Weingarten
1 Cathy at the crossroads 1965
2 Cathy's secret kingdom 1966

Farjeon, Eleanor
1 Martin Pippin in the apple orchard 1921
2 Martin Pippin in the daisy field 1937

Farley, Walter
1 The black stallion 1941
2 The black stallion returns 1945
3 Son of the black stallion 1950
4 The black stallion and Satan 1949
5 The blood bay colt 1950
6 The black stallion mystery 1957
7 The black stallion and Flame 1960
8 The black stallion's filly 1952
9 Little Black, a pony 1964
10 Little Black goes to the circus 1965
□
1 Amelioranne and the magic ring 1933
2 Amelioranne prize packet 1933
3 Amelioranne's washing day 1934
ISLAND STALLION SERIES:
1 The island stallion races 1955
2 The island stallion's fury 1951
3 The island stallion 1948
□
1 The black stallion revolts 1953
2 The black stallion's courage 1956
3 The black stallion's sulky colt 1954

Farmer, D.
1 The first big radio thin king book 1983
2 The second big radio thin king book 1983

Farmer, Penelope
CHARLOTTE AND EMMA MAKEPEACE:
1 The summer birds 1962
2 Emma in winter 1966
3 Charlotte sometimes 1969
□
1 The seagull 1965
2 Dragonfly summer 1971

Farrar, Frederic William
1 Darkness and dawn 1891
2 Gathering clouds 1895

Farrell, Anne
MITCHELL FAMILY:
1 The gift-wrapped pony 1977
2 The calf on Shale hill
3 Eight days at Guara
4 Shadow summer 1978

Farrimond, John
1 Graham's gang
2 The hills of heaven 1978

Farrow, George Edward
1 The Wallypug of Why 1895
2 The Wallypug in London 1898
3 Adventures in Wallypug-land 1904
4 The Wallypug in fog-land 1904
5 The Wallypug in the moon 1905
6 The Wallypug birthday book 1904
7 All about the Wallypug 1904
8 Wallypug tales 1904
9 Wallypug at play
10 In search of the Wallypug 1903
□
1 The little Panjandrum's dodo 1899
2 The new Panjandrum 1902
3 Adventures of a Dodo 1908

Fatchen, Max
THE MURRAY RIVER SERIES:
1 The river kings 1966
2 Conquest of the river 1970

Fatio, Louise
1 The happy lion 1955
2 The happy lion roars 1959
3 The three happy lions 1960
4 The happy lion's quest 1962
5 The happy lion in Africa 1963
6 The happy lion and the bear 1965
7 The happy lion's holiday 1968
8 The happy lion's treasure 1971
9 The happy lion's rabbits 1975
□
1 Hector penguin 1973
2 Hector and Christina 1978

Faulknor, Cliff
EAGLE CHILD, LATER WHITE BULL:
1 The white calf 1966
2 The white peril 1968
3 The smoke horse 1968

Fenwick, Jill
1 Mr Potter's garden
2 Mr Potter's parsnip 1978
3 Mr Potter and the parrots 1979

Ferguson, Ruby
1 Jill enjoys her ponies 1949
2 A stable for Jill 1951
3 Jill has two ponies 1952
4 Jill's gymkhana 1954
5 Jill's riding club 1956
6 Rosettes for Jill 1957
7 Jill and the perfect pony 1959
8 Pony jobs for Jill 1960
9 Jill's pony trek 1962

Ferra-Mikura, V., *see* **Mikura, Vera Ferra**

Fidler, Kathleen
THE BRYDONS SERIES:
1 The borrowed garden 1944
2 St. Jonathan's in the country 1945
3 The Brydons at Smuggler's Creek 1946
4 More adventures of the Brydons 1947
5 The Brydons go camping 1948
6 The Brydons in summer 1949
7 The Brydons do battle 1949
8 The Brydons in a pickle 1950
9 The Brydons look for trouble 1950
10 The Brydons hunt for treasure 1952
11 The Brydons catch queer fish 1952
12 The Brydons stick at nothing 1951
13 The Brydons abroad 1953
14 The Brydons get things going 1954
15 Surprise for the Brydons 1950
16 Challenge to the Brydons 1956
17 The Brydons at Blackpool 1960
18 The Brydons on the Broads 1955
19 The Brydons go canoeing 1963
□
1 Deans move in 1953
2 Deans follow a clue 1954
3 Deans solve a mystery 1954
4 Deans defy danger 1955
5 Deans dive for treasure 1956
6 Deans to the rescue 1957
7 Deans' lighthouse adventure 1959
8 Deans and Mr Popple 1960
9 Deans' Dutch adventure 1962
HERMITAGE SERIES:
1 Tales of the North Country 1952
2 Tales of London 1953
3 Tales of the Midlands 1954
4 Tales of the West Country 1961
□
1 The treasure of Ebba 1968
2 The gold of Fast Castle 1970

Fine, Anne
1 The summer-house loon 1978
2 The other, darker Ned 1979

Finkel, George
GROUP-CAPTAIN METCALFE SERIES:
1 Mystery of the secret beach 1960
2 Ship in hiding 1961
3 Cloudmaker 1962
4 The singing sands 1963
□
1 The stranded duck 1975
2 Operation Aladdin 1976

Finlay, Sir Campbell Kirkman
JOHN MACINNES SERIES:
1 Fisherman's gold 1961
2 Shepherd's purse 1963
3 Farewell to the Western Isles 1964

Finlay, Winifred
GILLIAN LINDSAY SERIES:
1 The Witch of Redesdale 1951
2 Peril in the Pennines 1953
3 Peril in Lakeland 1953
JUDITH NORTON SERIES:
1 Cotswold holiday 1954
2 Judith in Hanover 1955
3 The lost silver of Langdon 1955
4 Storm over Cheviot 1955
5 The lost emeralds of Black Howe 1965
6 Castle for four 1966
□
1 Canal holiday 1957
2 The cruise of the Susan 1958

Finney, Patricia
1 A shadow of gulls 1977
2 The crow goddess 1978

Firmin, Peter
BASIL BRUSH SERIES:
1 Basil Brush at the seaside 1969
2 Basil Brush goes boating 1969
3 Basil Brush goes flying 1969
4 Basil Brush in the jungle 1970

5 Basil Brush and a dragon 1971
6 Basil Brush finds treasure 1971
7 Basil Brush builds a house 1973
8 Basil Brush gets a medal 1973
9 Basil Brush on the trail 1979
10 Basil Brush and the windmills 1979

See also **Postgate O.** *and* **Firmin, P.**

Fisher, D., *see* **De Wito Series.**

Fisk, Nicholas

STARSTORMERS SERIES:
1 Flamers 1979
2 Starstormers 1980
3 Sunburst 1980
4 Evil eye 1982
5 Volcano 1983

Fisker, Robert
1 Sparrow falls out of the nest 1979
2 Sparrow flies away 1980

Fitzgerald, John Dennis
1 The great brain 1970
2 More adventures of the great brain 1972
3 Me and my little brain 1974
4 The great brain is back 1976

Fitzhugh, Louise

HARRIET M. WELSH:
1 Harriet the spy 1974
2 The long secret 1975

Fix, Philippe
1 The house that Beebo built 1969
2 Beebo and the Fizzmen 1972
3 Beebo and the funny machine 1973

Flack, Marjorie
1 Angus and the cat 1933
2 Angus and the ducks 1933
3 Angus and Topsy 1935
4 Angus and Wag-Tail-Bess 1935
5 Angus lost 1933

Fleischman, Sid
1 McBroom's wonderful one-acre farm 1975
2 Here comes McBroom 1976
3 McBroom and the great race 1981

□

1 The ghost in the noonday sun 1970
2 The ghost on a Saturday night 1975

Fleming, Ian

CHITTY-CHITTY-BANG-BANG THE MAGICAL CAR:
1 Adventure no. 1 1964
2 Adventure no. 2 1964
3 Adventure no. 3 1965

Foreman, Michael
1 Panda's puzzle 1977
2 Panda and the odd lion 1980

Forest, Antonia

THE MARLOW FAMILY SERIES:
1 Autumn term 1948
2 The Marlows and the traitor 1953
3 Falconer's lure 1957
4 End of term 1959
5 Peter's room 1961
6 The Thursday kidnapping 1963
7 The thuggery affair 1965
8 The ready-made family 1967
9 The cricket term 1974
10 The attic term 1976
11 Run away home 1982

□

1 The players' boy 1970
2 The players and the rebels 1971

Fowler, Richard
1 A book-full of beans 1978
2 A bus-full of beans 1979

Francoise, *pseud.* **[Francoise Seignoboce]**
1 Jeanne-Marie counts her sheep 1955
2 Jeanne-Marie in gay Paris 1957
3 Spring-time for Jeanne-Marie 1958
4 Jeanne-Marie at the fair 1959
5 The big rain 1961
6 Noel for Jeanne-Marie 1966

Franzen, Nils-Olof

AGATON SAX SERIES:
1 Agaton Sax and the diamond thieves 1967
2 Agaton Sax and the Scotland Yard mystery 1969
3 Agaton Sax and the Max Brothers 1970
4 Agaton Sax and the criminal doubles 1971

5 Agaton Sax and the Colossus of Rhodes 1972
6 Agaton Sax and the London computer plot 1973
7 Agaton Sax and the league of silent exploders 1974
8 Agaton and the haunted house 1975
9 Agaton Sax and the big rig 1976
10 Agaton Sax and Lispinton's grandfather clock 1978

Friskey, Margaret
1 Mystery of the magic meadows 1971
2 The mystery of Rackety's way 1972

Fry, Rosalie Kingsmill
1 Lucinda and the painted bell 1956
2 Lucinda and the sailor kitten 1959
3 Fly home Colombina 1960

Furminger, Jo
BLACKBIRD PONY GROUP:
1 A pony at Blackbird cottage 1975
2 Blackbirds ride a mystery trail 1976
3 Blackbird's pony trek 1977
4 Blackbirds and the gift pony 1978
5 Blackbirds own gymkhana 1979
6 Saddle up Blackbirds 1980
7 Blackbirds at the gallop 1980
□
1 A spell for Miss Grimsdike 1979
2 Mrs Boffy's birthday 1980
3 Oh no, Aunt Belladonna 1982

Furminger, Justine
1 Bobbie takes the reins 1981
2 Bobbie's sponsored ride 1982

Fyson, Jenny Grace
1 The three brothers of Ur 1964
2 The journey of the eldest son 1965

Gackenbach, Dick
1 Harrie rabbit 1977
2 Mother rabbit's son Tom 1978
3 Hattie be quiet, Harrie be good 1980
4 Hattie, Tom and the chicken witch 1981

Gallico, Paul
1 Jennie 1950
2 Thomasina 1957
□
1 The day the guinea pig talked 1962
2 The day Jean-Pierre was pidnapped 1963
3 The day Jean-Pierre went round the world 1965
4 The day Jean-Pierre joined the circus 1969

Garfield, Leon
1 The boy and the monkey 1969
2 The captain's watch 1972
3 Lucifer Wilkins 1973
Stories of the Southern USA before the Civil War. Republished in paperback as an omnibus edition under the title of 'I' 1976.
THE APPRENTICES SERIES:
1 The lamplighter's funeral 1976
2 Mirror, mirror 1976
3 Labour in vain 1977
4 The valentine 1977
5 Rosy Starling 1977
6 The foot 1977
7 The dumb cake 1977
8 The filthy beast 1978
9 The enemy 1978
'The Apprentices' 1982 is a collection of all the stories. A series of stories about London apprentices in the 18th century.
BOSTOCK AND HARRIS:
1 The strange affair of Adelaide Harris 1977
2 Bostock and Harris 1979
□
1 The God beneath the sea 1976 (with E. Bushen)
2 The golden shadow 1978
Stories of mythology.

Garis, Howard R.
1 Uncle Wiggily and the will-a-wong 1977
2 Uncle Wiggily and his woodland friends 1977
3 Uncle Wiggily and the pirates and other stories 1978
4 Uncle Wiggily and the strange notes and other stories 1978

Garland, Sarah
1 Rose and her bath 1970
2 Rose, the bath and the mer boy 1972

Garner, Alan
1 The weirdstone of Brisingamen 1960
2 The moon of Gomrath 1963
THE STONE BOOK QUARTET:
1 The stone book 1976
2 Tom Fobble's day 1977
3 Grannie Reardun 1977
4 The Aimer gate 1978
Also available as one volume under the title 'The Stone book'.

Garnett, Eve
RUGGLES FAMILY SERIES:
1 The family from One-End Street 1937
2 Further adventures of the family from One-End Street 1956
3 Holiday at the Dew Drop Inn 1962
4 A Christmas at One-End Street (a short story in 'Lost and Found') 1974

Garrard, Phillis
1 Hilda at school 1929
2 The doings of Hilda 1932
3 Hilda's adventures 1936
4 Hilda, fifteen 1944
'New Zealand schoolgirl' 1958 is an omnibus volume of 1-3.

Gascoigne, Bamber *and* **Christine**
1 Fearless Freddy's sunken treasure 1982
2 Fearless Freddy's magic wish 1982

Gathorne-Hardy, I., *see* **Hardy, Jonathan Gathorne-**

Gervaise, Mary
'G' FOR GEORGIA SERIES:
1 A pony of your own 1950
2 Ponies and holidays 1950
3 Ponies in clover 1952
4 Ponies and mysteries 1953
5 Pony from the farm 1954
6 Pony clue 1955
7 Pony island 1957
8 Vanishing pony 1958
9 A puzzle for ponies 1964
10 Secret of pony pass 1965
MARSTON CHILDREN SERIES:
1 Golden path adventure 1955
2 Secret of Golden path 1956
3 Strangers at Golden path 1958
4 Golden path pets 1957
FARTHINGALE SERIES:
1 Fireworks at Farthingale 1954
2 The Farthingale fete 1955
3 Farthingale feud 1957
4 Farthingale find 1960
BELINDA SERIES:
1 A pony for Belinda 1959
2 Belinda rides to school 1960
3 Belinda's other pony 1961
4 Belinda wins her spurs 1962

Gibson, Gloria
1 Maise in the attic 1980
2 Maise in school 1983

Gifford, Griselda
1 The youngest Taylor 1964
2 Ben's expedition 1965
□
1 Jenny and the sheep thieves 1975
2 Mirabelle's secret 1976

Gilman, Robert
1 The rebel of Rhada 1970
2 The navigator of Rhada 1971

Gilmore, D. H.
1 Adventures of Catkin and Codlin, Christopher Cricket and Benjamin Bumble 1978
2 Adventures of Anthony Ant and the earwig pirates, Gregory Grasshopper and the cruise of the saucy walnut 1979
3 Adventures of Drowsy the Drone, Cuthbert the caterpillar and Wilfred the Wasp and the lost ladybirds 1981

Gilroy, Beryl
YOUNG ROY SERIES:
1 New people at twenty four 1974
2 A visitor from home 1974
3 Knock at Mrs Herbs' 1974

Gladstone, Josephine *and* **Binder, Pearl**
1 Chi Ming and the tiger kitten
2 Chi Ming and the lion dance
3 Chi Ming and the jade earring 1974

Godden, Margaret Rumer
1 Miss Happiness and Miss Flower 1961
2 Little Plum 1963

Golden Gorse, *pseud.* **[M. A. Wace]**
1 Moorland Mousie 1929
2 Older Mousie 1931

Goldsmith, John
1 Mrs Babcary goes to sea 1980
2 Mrs Babcary goes to town 1980
3 Mrs Babcary goes West 1980
4 Mrs Babcary's driving machine 1981
5 Mrs Babcary's steam cart 1981
6 Mrs Babcary's treat 1981

Goodall, John
PADDY PORK SERIES:
1 Jacko
2 The midnight adventures of Kelly, Dot and Esmerelda
3 Shrewnettina's birthday
4 Paddy's evening out
5 Creepy castle
6 Paddy Pork's holiday
7 Naughty Nancy the bad bridesmaid
8 The surprise picnic
9 The adventures of Paddy Pork 1980
10 The ballooning adventures of Paddy Pork 1980
11 Paddy's new hut 1980
12 Paddy finds a job 1981
13 Paddy goes travelling 1982
14 Paddy Pork—odd jobs

Goodwin, Tim
1 The ring of spears 1979
2 The silver hoard 1980

Goolden, Barbara
THE TABOR FAMILY:
1 Minty 1961
2 Five pairs of hands 1962
3 Minty and the missing picture 1963
4 Minty and the secret room 1964
5 Trouble for the Tabors 1966
6 Top secret 1969

Gordon, Margaret
1 Wilberforce goes on a picnic 1982
2 Wilberforce goes shopping 1983

Goscinny, Rene *and* **Morris**
LUCKY LUKE SERIES:
1 Jesse James 1972
2 The stage coach 1972
3 Dalton City 1973
4 The tenderfoot 1973
5 Western circus 1974
'Ma Dalton' and 'Canyon Apache' have been published in French editions only.

Goscinny, Rene *and* **Sempe, J. J.**
1 Nicholas and the gang at school 1977
2 Nicholas and the gang again 1977
3 Nicholas on holiday 1978
4 Nicholas and the gang 1978
5 Nicholas at large 1979

Goscinny, Rene *and* **Uderzo, Albert**
1 Asterix the Gaul 1969
2 Asterix and Cleopatra 1969
3 Asterix the gladiator 1969
4 Asterix in Britain 1970
5 Asterix the legionary 1970
6 Asterix and the big fight 1971
7 Asterix in Spain 1971
8 Asterix at the Olympic games 1972
9 Asterix and the Roman agent 1972
10 Asterix in Switzerland 1973
11 The mansions of the gods 1973
12 Asterix and the Goths 1973
13 Asterix and the laurel wreath 1974
14 Asterix and the soothsayer 1975
15 Asterix and the golden sickle 1975
16 Asterix and the great crossing 1976
17 Asterix and the cauldron 1976
18 Asterix and the chieftain's shield 1977
19 Asterix Caesar's gift 1977
20 Asterix and the Normans 1978
21 Obelix and co 1978
22 The twelve tasks of Asterix 1978
23 Asterix and the banquet 1979
24 Asterix in Belgium 1980
25 Asterix and the great divide 1981
26 Asterix in Corsica 1980
27 Asterix and the black gold 1982
28 Asterix and son 1983
□
1 Dogmatix and the boar hunt 1973
2 Dogmatix and the storm 1973
3 Dogmatix and the well-deserved tea-party 1974
4 Dogmatix makes a friend 1974
5 Dogmatix and the ugly little eagle 1983
6 Dogmatix and the magic potions 1983

Graham, Margaret Bloy
1 Benjy and the barking bird 1973
2 Benjy's dog house 1974

Gramatky, Hardie
1 Little Toot 1946
2 Little Toot on the Thames 1965
3 Little Toot on the Grand canal 1967
4 Little Toot on the Mississippi 1974
5 Little Toot through the golden gate 1977

Grant, Gwen
1 Private Keep Out! 1978
2 Knock and wait 1979
3 One way only 1983

Grant, John
1 Littlenose 1968
2 Littlenose moves house 1969
3 Littlenose the hero 1971
4 Littlenose the hunter 1972
5 Littlenose the fisherman 1973
6 Littlenose to the rescue 1974
7 Littlenose's birthday 1979
8 Littlenose the marksman 1982
9 Littlenose the leader 1977
The above were published in paperback, 1-3 were published in hardback as 'The adventures of Littlenose' 1972 and 4-6 as 'More adventures of Littlenose' 1976.

Gray, Dulcie *see* **Roger Moore and the Crime Fighters series**

Greaves, Margaret
1 Charlie, Emma and Alberic 1980
2 Charlie, Emma and the dragon family 1982

Gree, Gerard *and* **Gree, Alain**
1 Little Tom makes ten discoveries 1978
2 Little Tom learns about time 1978
3 Little Tom and some animal friends 1978
4 Little Tom protects the environment 1978

Green, Candida Lycott
1 The adventures of Hadrian the hedgehog 1967
2 Hadrian in the Orient 1969

Green, Cliff
1 The incredible steam driven adventures of Riverboat Bill 1979
2 The further adventures of Riverboat Bill 1982

Green, Roger Lancelyn
THE SPEARLAKE CHILDREN SERIES:
1 The wonderful stranger 1950
2 The luck of the Lunns 1952
3 Theft of the golden cat 1955

Greene, Bette
1 Summer of my German soldier 1974
2 Morning is a long time coming 1978
□
1 Phillip Hall likes me I reckon maybe 1974
2 Get on out of here Phillip Hall 1982

Grender, Iris
1 The first did I ever tell you book 1976
2 The second did I ever tell you book 1978
3 The third did I ever tell you book 1980
4 Did I ever tell you about my Irish Great Grandmother? 1981
5 Did I ever tell you about my birthday party? 1983

Gretz, Susanna
1 Teddybears 1-10 1969
2 The bears who stayed indoors 1970
3 The bears who went to the seaside 1972
4 Teddybears ABC 1974
5 Teddybears cookbook 1978
6 Teddybears moving day 1981
7 Teddybears go shopping 1982

Grimm, Geraldine
1 King Goblin and his forest friends 1972
2 King Goblin and his golden treasure 1972
3 King Goblin loses his throne 1973
4 King Goblin returns 1973

Grimwade, Peter *see* **Doctor Who Series**

Gripe, Harald *and* **Gripe, Maria**
HUGO AND JOSEPHINE TRILOGY:
1 Hugo and Josephine 1969
2 Josephine 1971
3 Hugo 1971
□

1 The night daddy 1971
2 Julia's house 1975
□
1 Elvis and his secret 1976
2 Elvis and his friends 1978
3 The real Elvis

Gruelle, Johnny

RAGGEDY ANN SERIES:

1 Raggedy Ann and Raggedy Ann's very own fairy stories 1975
2 Raggedy Ann stories 1975
3 Raggedy Ann's magical wishes 1976
4 Raggedy Ann and the camel with wrinkled knees 1976
5 Raggedy Ann and Andy 1978
6 Raggedy Ann and the hobby horse 1978

Raggedy Ann has been a favourite in America for many years and was first published in the U.K. in 1975.

Guy, Rosa

1 The friends 1974
2 Edith Guy 1979
3 Ruby 1976

Gydal, Monica

OLLY SEES IT THROUGH SERIES:

1 When Olly's grandad died 1976
2 When Gemma's parents got divorced 1976
3 When Olly went to hospital 1976
4 When Olly got a little brother 1976
5 When Olly saw an accident 1977
6 When Olly moved house 1977

Hadfield, Alice Mary

THE WILLIVER CHRONICLES:

1 Williver's luck 1964
2 Williver's quest 1965
3 Williver's return 1967

Haigh, Sheila

1 Watch for the ghost 1975
2 Watch for smoke 1978
3 Watch for the champion 1979
4 Watch for danger 1983

Hale, Kathleen

ORLANDO, THE MARMALADE CAT SERIES:

1 Orlando's camping holiday 1938
2 Orlando's evening out 1941
3 Orlando's home life 1942
4 Orlando, the marmalade cat buys a farm 1942
5 Orlando's silver wedding 1944
6 Orlando, the marmalade cat becomes a doctor 1944
7 Orlando's invisible pyjamas 1974
8 Orlando, the marmalade cat's trip abroad 1949
9 Orlando, the marmalade cat keeps a dog 1949
10 Orlando the judge 1950
11 Orlando, the marmalade cat, a seaside holiday 1952
12 Orlando's zoo 1954
13 Orlando's magic carpet 1958
14 Orlando, the marmalade cat and the frisky housewife 1956
15 Orlando, the marmalade cat buys a cottage 1963
16 Orlando and the three graces 1965
17 Orlando goes to the moon 1968
18 Orlando, the marmalade cat and the water cats 1972
□
1 Henrietta, the faithful hen 1943
2 Henrietta's magic egg 1973

Hale, Sylvia

1 Caroline takes to dancing 1960
2 Caroline joins the stars 1961
□
1 Painter's mate 1964
2 Mystery boxes 1965

Hall, M., *joint author, see* **Cosgrove, Brian** *and* **Hall, M.**

Hall, Malcolm

1 Headlines
2 Forecast 1979

Hall, Willis

HOLLINS FAMILY:

1 Henry Hollins and the dinosaur 1979
2 The summer of the dinosaur
3 The last vampire 1982

Hall, Willis, *see* **Waterhouse, Keith** *and* **Hall, Willis,** *joint authors*

Hallett, Phyllis

CARLISLE FAMILY SERIES:

1 The white galloper
2 Jumping cats 1977

Hamilton, Virginia

1 Justice and her brothers 1979
2 Dustland 1980
3 The gathering 1981

Hamre, L.

PETER HORDEN SERIES:

1 Otter three two calling 1961
2 Blue two bale-out 1961
3 Ready for take-off 1962

Hardcastle, Michael

BANK VALE UNITED:

1 In the net 1971
2 United 1973
3 Away from home 1974
4 Free kick 1974

SCORTON ROVERS:

1 Soccer is also a game 1960
2 Shoot on sight 1967

MARK FOX:

1 Mark Fox Vol. 1; The first goal 1980
2 Mark Fox Vol. 2; Breakaway 1980
3 Mark Fox Vol. 3; On the ball 1980
4 Mark Fox Vol. 4; Shooting star 1982

□

1 The Saturday horse 1977
2 The switch horse 1979

□

1 Goals in the air 1972
2 Where the action is
3 Top of the league 1979

Stories about Kenny, a young football star. Titles in the Pyramid book series for teenage readers.

□

1 Roar to victory 1982
2 Fast from the gate 1983

□

1 Crash car 1977
2 Strong arm 1977
3 Fire on the sea 1977
4 Holiday house 1977

Stories about Steve and Anna; Inner ring hipsters for teenagers.

Hardy, Jonathan Gathorne

1 Jane's adventures in and out of the book 1966
2 Jane's adventures on the island of Peeg 1968
3 Jane's adventures in a balloon 1975

□

1 Terrible kidnapping of Cyril Bonhamy 1978
2 Cyril Bonhamy versus Madam Big 1981
3 Cyril Bonhamy and the great drain robbery 1983

Hargreaves, Roger

HIPPO, POTTO AND MOUSE:

1 Hippo, leaves home 1976
2 Hippo, Potto and Mouse 1976
3 Mouse gets caught 1976
4 Potto finds a job 1976

LITTLE MISS SERIES:

1 Little Miss Bossy 1981
2 Little Miss Helpful 1981
3 Little Miss Late 1981
4 Little Miss Naughty 1981
5 Little Miss Neat 1981
6 Little Miss Plump 1981
7 Little Miss Scatterbrain 1981
8 Little Miss Shy 1981
9 Little Miss Splendid 1981
10 Little Miss Sunshine 1981
11 Little Miss Tiny 1981
12 Little Miss Trouble 1981

MR MEN SERIES:

1 Mr Bump 1971
2 Mr Greedy 1971
3 Mr Happy 1971
4 Mr Sneeze 1971
5 Mr Slow 1971
6 Mr Nosey 1971
7 Mr Daydream 1972
8 Mr Silly 1972
9 Mr Small 1972
10 Mr Uppity 1972
11 Mr Bounce 1976
12 Mr Chatterbox 1976
13 Mr Dizzy 1976
14 Mr Forgetful 1976
15 Mr Funny 1976
16 Mr Fussy 1976
17 Mr Impossible 1976
18 Mr Jelly 1976
19 Mr Mean 1976

20 Mr Men's Christmas 1976
21 Mr Men on holiday 1976
22 Mr Muddle 1976
23 Mr Noisy 1976
24 Mr Strong 1976
25 Mr Men's sports' day 1977
26 Mr Small's colouring book 1977
27 Mr Busy 1978
28 Mr Clumsy 1978
29 Mr Clever 1978
30 Mr Grumpy 1979
31 Mr Mischief 178
32 Mr Nonsense 1978
33 Mr Quiet 1978
34 Mr Rush 1978
35 Mr Skinny 1978
36 Mr Worry 1978
37 Mr Greedy at the shops 1979
38 Mr Happy at the seaside 1979
39 Mr Silly at the farm 1979
40 Mr Tickle in the park 1979
41 Mr Trumpet 1979
42 Mr Trumpet's fruit 1979
43 Mr Funny at the circus 1980
44 Mr Muddle goes to school 1980
45 Mr Nosey follows his nose 1980
46 Mr Strong to the rescue 1980
'My own Mr Men storybook' 1978, 'Second Mr Men storybook' 1979, 'My very own Mr Men storybook' 1979, 'Mr Men ABC' 1978, 'Mr Men Annual' 1979. Various other titles in the series.

□

1 Roar 1979
2 Roar's day of mistakes 1981

□

1 Moo 1979
2 Moo's fancy hats 1981

□

1 Neigh 1979
2 Neigh moves house

Harman, C.

1 Tales told to an African crocodile
2 More tales told to an African crocodile

Harnett, Cynthia

1 Ring out, Bow Bells, 1953
2 The writing on the hearth 1971
3 The load of unicorn 1959
Not precisely sequels but a connected historical sequence. In 2 and 3 Caxton is the main character. The above is chronological order.

Harris, Geraldine

KERISH-LO-TAAN'S QUEST:

1 Prince of the Godborn: seven citadels Part 1 1982
2 The children of the wind: seven citadels Part 2 1982
3 Dead kingdom: seven citadels Part 3 1983
4 The seventh gate: seven citadels Part 4 1983

Harris, Joel Chandler

1 The story of Aaron 1896
2 Aaron in the Wildwoods 1898

□

1 Uncle Remus of the old plantation 1881 (Uncle Remus: his songs and sayings)
2 Nights with Uncle Remus 1883
3 Uncle Remus and his friends 1892
4 The Tar-baby and other rhymes of Uncle Remus 1904
5 Uncle Remus and Brer Rabbit 1907
6 Uncle Remus returns 1918
These are the original volumes. Collections have been published under several different titles. 'The Chronicles of Aunt Minery Ann' consists of tales told by a sister of Uncle Remus.

Harris, John

MARTIN FALCONER:

1 The fledglings 1972
2 The Professionals 1973
3 The victors 1975
4 The interceptors 1978
5 The revolutionaries 1978

Harris, Leon

MAURICE THE MOUSE:

1 The great picture robbery 1967
2 Maurice goes to sea 1969

Harris, Ray

1 The adventures of Turkey 1958
2 Turkey and partners 1959
3 Turkey and Co. 1961

Harris, Rosemary
THE STORY OF REUBEN, EGYPTIAN TRILOGY:
1 The moon in the cloud 1968
2 The shadow on the sun 1970
3 The bright and morning star 1972
□
1 A quest for Orion 1978
2 Tower of the stars 1980

Hastings, Valerie
1 Jo and the skiffle group 1958
2 Jo and Coney's cavern 1959
3 Jo and the jumping boy 1960

Hatch, Richard Warren
1 The curious lobster 1937
2 The curious lobster's island 1940

Hatcher, Josephine
1 The Gasworks Alley gang 1960
2 The Gasworks Alley gang goes west 1961

Hatfield, John
1 Quintilian 1968
2 Quintilian and the curious weather shop 1969
3 Quintilian meets Mr Punch 1970

Hauptmann, Tatjana
1 A day in the life of Petronella Pig 1979
2 Hurray for Peregrine Pig 1980

Hawthorne, Nathaniel
1 A wonder book for boys and girls 1852
2 Tanglewood tales 1853

Hayes, Richard
1 The secret army 1977
2 The xenon file 1980

Hayes, Brian, *see* **Doctor Who series**

Haywood, Carolyn
1 'B' is for Betsy 1939
2 Betsy and Billy 1941
3 Back to school with Betsy 1943
4 Betsy and the boys 1945
5 Betsy's little star 1950
6 Betsy and the circus 1954
7 Betsy's busy summer 1956
8 Betsy's winterhouse 1958
9 Snowbound with Betsy 1962
10 Betsy and Mr Kilpatrick 1967
□
1 Little Eddie 1947
2 Eddie and the fire engine 1949
3 Eddie and the gardenia 1951
4 Eddie's pay dirt 1953
5 Eddie and his big deals 1955
6 Eddie makes music 1957
7 Eddie and Lovella 1959
8 Annie Pat and Eddie 1960
9 Eddie's green thumb 1964
10 Eddie the dog holder 1966
11 Ever-ready Eddie 1968
12 Eddie's happening 1971
□
1 Here's a Penny 1944
2 Penny and Peter 1946
3 Penny goes to camp 1948

Heide, Florence Parry
1 The shrinking of Treehorn 1971
2 Treehorn's treasure 1981

Held, J.
1 Richard and Valerie in the garden 1970
2 Richard and Valerie in the mountains 1970
3 Richard and Valerie on the farm 1970

Hellberg, Hans-Eric
1 Marie 1974
2 Marie and Martin 1975
3 I am Marie 1978

Hellner, Katarina
1 Joan is sad 1979
2 Joan is scared 1979
3 Joan is angry 1979
4 Joan is happy 1979
Picture books showing a child's emotional reactions to the world around her.

Henry, Marguerite
1 Misty of Chincoteague 1961
2 Stormy, Misty's foal 1965

Hentoff, Nat
1 This school is driving me crazy 1977
2 Does this school have capital punishment 1982

Henty, George Alfred

DUTCH REPUBLIC SERIES:

1 By pike and dyke 1890
2 By England's aid 1891

PENINSULAR WAR SERIES:

1 With Moore at Corunna 1909
2 Under Wellington's command 1899

THIRTY YEARS WAR SERIES:

1 The lion of the north 1886
2 Won by the sword 1900

Not strictly sequels, but of the many Henty titles, the above are concerned with the same historical periods.

Herbert, R.

1 Rufus tractor 1969
2 Rufus rolls on 1971

Herge, *pseud.* **[G. Remi]**

TINTIN SERIES:

1 The crab with the golden claws 1959
2 King Ottokar's sceptre 1958
3 The secret of the unicorn 1959
4 Red Rackam's treasure 1959
5 Destination moon 1959
6 Explorers on the moon 1959
7 The Calculus affair 1960
8 The red sea sharks 1960
9 The shooting star 1961
10 Tintin in Tibet 1962
11 The seven crystal balls 1962
12 Prisoners of the sun 1962
13 The Castafiore emeralds 1963
14 The black island 1966
15 Flight 714 1968
16 Cigars of the Pharoah 1971
17 Land of black gold 1972
18 Tintin and the lake of sharks 1973
19 Tintin and the broken ear 1975
20 Tintin and the Picaros 1976
21 Tintin and the golden fleece 1976
22 The blue lotus 1983

There are sequels within the series, e.g. 3 and 4, 5 and 6. No. 18 is based on the Herge characters, being adapted from a film.

Herman, H.

1 The forest princess 1976
2 The return of the forest princess 1976

Herrman, Frank

1 The giant Alexander 1964
2 The giant Alexander and the circus 1966
3 The giant Alexander in America 1968
4 The giant Alexander and Hannibal the elephant 1971

Heward, Constance

1 Ameliaranne and the green umbrella 1920
2 Ameliaranne keeps shop 1928
3 Ameliaranne, cinema star 1929
4 Ameliaranne in town 1930
5 Ameliaranne at the circus 1931
6 Ameliaranne and the big treasure 1932
7 Ameliaranne and the prize packet 1933
8 Ameliaranne's washing day 1934
9 Ameliaranne at the zoo 1936
10 Ameliaranne at the farm 1937
11 Ameliaranne gives a Christmas party 1938
12 Ameliaranne camps out 1939
13 Ameliaranne keeps school 1940
14 Ameliaranne gives a concert 1940
15 Ameliaranne goes touring 1941
16 Ameliaranne and the jumble sale 1943
17 Ameliaranne bridesmaid 1946
18 Ameliaranne goes digging 1948
19 Ameliaranne's moving day 1950

Not all the titles are by Heward. 6 is by N. Joan, 7 and 8 by E. Farjeon, 9 by K. L. Thompson, 14 by M. Gilmour, 16 by E. Osborne, 17 and 19 by E. Morris and 18 by L. Wood.

Hicks, Clifford Byron

1 Alvin Fernald, mayor for a day 1974
2 Alvin Fernald, superweasel 1975

Hildick, Edmond Wallace

THE MCGURK ORGANISATION:

1 Dolls in danger 1974
2 The nose knows 1974
3 The case of the condemned cat 1975
4 The case of the menaced midget 1975
5 The case of the nervous newsboy 1975
6 The great rabbit robbery 1976
7 The case of the invisible dog 1977
8 The case of the secret scribbler 1978
9 The case of the phantom frog 1979
10 The case of the treetop treasure 1980

□

1 Jim Starling 1958
2 Jim Starling and the agency 1958
3 Jim Starling's holiday 1960
4 Jim Starling and the colonel 1960
5 Jim Starling goes to town 1963
6 Jim Starling takes over 1963
7 Jim Starling and the spotted dog 1963

□

1 Birdy Jones 1967
2 Birdy and the group 1968
3 Birdy swings north 1969
4 Birdy in Amsterdam 1970
5 Birdy Jones and the New York Heads 1974

□

1 The Questers 1966
2 Calling Questers four 1967
3 The Questers and the whispering spy 1967

□

1 Meet Lemon Kelly 1963
2 Lemon Kelly dig's deep 1964
3 Lemon Kelly and the home-made boy 1968

□

1 Luvie's lot 1965
2 Luvie's S.O.S. 1968
3 Luvie's snowstorm 1975

Hill, Douglas

KEILL RANDOR SERIES:

1 Galactic warlord 1979
2 Deathwing over Veynga 1980
3 Day of the starwind 1980
4 Planet of the warlord 1981
5 Young legionary 1982

FINN FERRALL SERIES:

1 The Huntsman 1982
2 Warriors of the wasteland 1983

Hill, Eric

1 Where's Spot? 1980
2 Spot's first walk 1981
3 Spot's birthday party 1983
4 Spot's first Christmas 1983

Hill, Lorna

MARJORIE SERIES:

1 Marjorie and Co. 1948
2 Stolen holiday 1948
3 Border Peel
4 No medals for Guy 1962

PATIENCE SERIES:

1 They called her Patience 1951
2 It was all through Patience 1952
3 Castle in Northumbria 1953
4 So Guy came too 1954
5 The five shilling holiday 1955

ANNETTE DANCES SERIES:

1 Dancing Peel 1952
2 Dancer's luck 1955
3 Little dancer 1956
4 Dancer in the wings 1958
5 Dancer in danger 1959
6 Dancer on holiday 1961

SADLERS WELLS SERIES:

1 A dream of Sadlers Wells 1950
2 Veronica at the Wells 1951
3 Masquerade at the Wells 1952
4 No castanets at the Wells 1953
5 Jane leaves the Wells 1953
6 Ella at the Wells 1954
7 Return to the Wells 1955
8 Principal role 1957
9 Susan fearless
10 Dress-rehearsal 1959
11 Back-stage 1960
12 Vicki in Venice 1962
13 The secret 1964

THE VICARAGE CHILDREN SERIES:

1 The Vicarage children 1961
2 More about Mandy 1963
3 The Vicarage children in Skye 1966

Hinchcliffe, Philip, *see* **Doctor Who Series**

Hinton, Nigel

1 Beaver towers 1980
2 The witch's revenge 1981

Hitchcock, Alfred, *editor*

THREE INVESTIGATORS SERIES:

1 Secret of terror castle
2 Mystery of the stuttering parrot
3 Mystery of the whispering mummy
4 Mystery of the green ghost
5 Mystery of the vanishing treasure
6 The secret of Skeleton Island
7 Mystery of the fiery eye
8 Mystery of the silver spider
9 Mystery of the screaming clock
10 Mystery of the moaning cave
11 Mystery of the talking skull
12 Mystery of the laughing shadow

13 The secret of the crooked cat
14 Mystery of the coughing dragon
15 Mystery of the flaming footprint
16 Mystery of the nervous lion
17 Mystery of the singing serpent
18 Mystery of the shrinking house
19 Mystery of the monster mountain
20 The secret of Phantom Lake
21 The secret of the haunted mirror
22 The mystery of the dead man's riddle
23 Mystery of the invisible dog 1976
24 The mystery of the dancing devil 1977
25 The mystery of the headless horse 1978
26 The mystery of the deadly double
27 The secret of shark reef
Although the name of Alfred Hitchcock is associated with the series, titles are by various authors.

Hoare, R. J.
ROBBY OF THE GLOBE SERIES:
1 Sinister hoard 1958
2 Desperate venture 1959
3 Secret in the Sahara 1960

Hoban, Lillian
1 Arthur's Christmas cookies 1974
2 Arthur's honey bear 1975
3 Arthur's pen pal 1977
4 Arthur's prize reader 1979
5 Arthur's funny money 1982

Hoban, Russell Conwell
1 Bedtime for Frances 1960
2 A baby sister for Frances 1964
3 Bread and jam for Frances 1964
4 A birthday for Frances 1968
5 Best friends for Frances 1969
6 A bargain for Frances 1970
7 Egg thoughts and other Frances songs 1972
□
1 How Tom beat Captain Najork and his hired sportsman 1974
2 A near thing for Captain Najork 1975
□
1 Dinner at Albertas' 1973
2 Arthur's new power 1980
□
1 They came from Aargh! 1981
2 The hungry three 1982
3 Flight of Bembel Rudzuk 1982
4 Battle of Zormla 1982
5 The battle of Zormia 1983

Hodges, Cyril Walter
THE STORY OF KING ALFRED
1 The namesake 1964
2 The Marsh King 1967

Hoff, C.
1 Johnny Texas 1950
2 Johnny Texas on the San Antonio road 1953
Stories of the early days of Texas

Hofmeyer, Hans
1 Garibaldi's ski-boat 1960
2 Fly away Paul 1963

Hogarth, Grace
HELEN HAMILTON:
1 The funny guy 1975
2 A sister for Helen 1976

Hogg, G.
1 Explorers awheel 1938
2 Explorers on the wall 1939
3 Explorers afloat 1940
JONTY SERIES:
1 Sealed orders 1948
2 The secret of Hollow Hill 1950
3 Norwegian journey 1951
4 Norwegian holiday 1952
5 Riddle of Dooley Castle 1953
6 The granite men 1954

Holden, Philip
1 Fawn 1976
2 Stag 1980
3 White patch 1982

Holland, Kevin Crossley
1 The sea stranger 1973
2 The fire-brother 1974
3 The earth-father 1976
Historical novels of the story of Wulf, a Saxon boy, and a Northumbrian missionary.

Holman, Felice
1 Elizabeth the treasure hunter 1967
2 Elizabeth the bird watcher 1967
3 Elizabeth and the marsh mystery 1967

Holt, Debden, *see* **Roger Moore and the crime fighters series**

Hope, Laura Lee

1 Bobbsey twins at school 1913
2 Bobbsey twins at the circus 1932
3 Bobbsey twins at the seashore 1907
4 Bobbsey twins on a houseboat 1915
5 Bobbsey twins in the country 1907
6 Bobbsey twins camping out 1955
7 Bobbsey twins wonderful secret 1931
8 Bobbsey twins solve a mystery 1934
9 Bobbsey twins at Meadow Brook 1915
10 Bobbsey twins at Snow Lodge 1913
11 Bobbsey twins on Blueberry Island 1945
12 Bobbsey twins at Lighthouse Point 1939
13 Bobbsey twins in Echo Valley 1943
14 Bobbsey twins in Eskimo land 1936
15 Bobbsey twins on the pony trail 1944
16 Bobbsey twins at Big Bear Pond 1953
17 Bobbsey twins at Sugar Maple Hill 1946
18 Bobbsey twins treasure hunting 1929
19 Bobbsey twins on a bicycle trip 1954
20 Bobbsey twins and the horse-shoe riddle 1953
21 Bobbsey twins at Mystery Mansion 1945
22 Bobbsey twins at Whitesail harbor 1952
23 Bobbsey twins in Rainbow Valley 1950
24 Bobbsey twins at Pilgrim Rock
25 Bobbsey twins at the Tower of London
26 Bobbsey twins' forest adventure
27 Bobbsey twins' own little ferryboat
28 Bobbsey twins at Indian Hollow 1940
29 Bobbsey twins in the mystery cave
30 Bobbsey twins in Tulip land 1949
31 Bobbsey twins' own little road 1951
32 Bobbsey twins at the ice carnival 1941
33 Bobbsey twins' big adventure at home
34 Bobbsey twins in a great city 1917

Hoppner, B. Bartos-

1 The Cossacks 1962
2 Save the Khan 1963

Huddy, Delia

1 Sandwich Street Blue
2 Sandwich Street Safari 1977
3 Creaky knees 1978

LUKE CRANTOCK SERIES:

1 Time piper 1976
2 The Humboldt effect 1982

INNER RING HIPSTERS SERIES:

1 Blow up 1978
2 Gate crashers 1978
3 Hush-a-bye-baby 1978
4 No ladder for Tom Bates 1978

Hughes, Fielden, *see* **Roger Moore and the crime fighters series**

Hughes, Monica

THE ISIS TRILOGY:

1 The keeper of the Isis light 1980
2 The Guardian of Isis 1981
3 The Isis pedlar 1982

□

1 Crisis on Conshelf 10 1975
2 Earthdark 1977

Hughes, Shirley

1 Lucy and Tom's day 1960
2 Lucy and Tom go to school 1973
3 Lucy and Tom at the seaside 1976
4 Lucy and Tom's Christmas 1981

□

1 Alfie gets in first 1981
2 Alfie's feet 1982
3 Alfie gives a hand 1983

□

1 Here comes Charlie Moon 1980
2 Charlie Moon and the big bonanza bust-up 1982

Hughes, Thomas

1 Tom Brown's schooldays 1857
2 Tom Brown at Oxford 1861

Hulke, Malcolm, *see* **Roger Moore and the crime fighters series** *and* **Doctor Who series**

Hunt, R.

1 Chutney and the fossil 1977
2 Chutney on the river 1977
3 Chutney at the circus 1977
4 Chutney and the new boy 1977
5 Chutney on the beach 1977
6 Chutney in the snow 1977

Hunter, Mollie

1 A sound of chariots 1973
2 The dragonfly years 1983

Hunter, Norman

THE KINGDOM OF INCREDIBLANIA:

1 The dribblesome teapot and other incredible stories 1969
2 The home-made dragon and other incredible stories 1971
3 The frantic phantom and other incredible stories 1973
4 Dust up at the royal disco 1975
5 Count Bakwerdz on the carpet and other incredible stories 1979
6 Sneeze and be slain and other incredible stories 1980

□

1 The incredible adventures of Professor Branestawm 1933
2 Professor Branestawm's treasure hunt and other incredible adventures 1937
3 Stories of Professor Branestawm 1939
4 The peculiar triumph of Professor Branestawm 1970
5 Professor Branestawm up the pole 1972
6 Professor Branestawm's dictionary 1973
7 Professor Branestawm's great revolution 1974
8 Professor Branestawm's compendium of puzzles 1975
9 Professor Branestawm's do-it-yourself handbook 1976
10 Professor Branestawm round the bend 1977
11 Professor Branestawm's perilous pudding 1979
12 Professor Branestawm and the wild letters 1980
13 Professor Branestawm's pocket motor car 1980
14 Professor Branestawm's building bust up 1982
15 Professor Branestawm's Mouse War 1982
16 Professor Branestawm's crunchy crockery 1983
17 Professor Branestawm's hair-raising idea 1983

'The best of Branestawm' 1980, an omnibus collection of stories, including tricks, puzzles, riddles, etc. 6, 8 and 9 are non-fiction.

Hurd, E. T.

1 Johnny Lion's book 1966
2 Johnny Lion's bad day 1971
3 Johnny Lion's rubber boots 1973

□

1 Catfish 1975
2 Catfish and the kidnapped cat 1976

Hurt, F. M.

PINETOPS SERIES:

1 The wonderful birthday 1954
2 Fun next door 1955
3 Two to make friends 1955
4 The exciting summer 1956
5 Thirteen for luck 1957
6 Intruders at Pinetops 1958

□

1 Crab Island 1965
2 Benny and the dolphin 1968

Hutchins, Pat

1 The house that sailed away 1976
2 Follow that bus 1977
3 The Mona Lisa mystery 1981

□

1 Titch 1972
2 You'll soon grow into them Titch 1983

Hyman, Robin

1 Casper and the lion cub 1974
2 Casper and the rainbow bird 1975

Ichikawa, Satomi

1 Suzanne and Nicholas in the garden 1977
2 Suzanne and Nicholas at the market 1977
3 Suzanne and Nicholas and the four seasons 1978

Ionesco, I.

JOSETTE SERIES:

1 Story no. 1
2 Story no. 2
3 Story no. 3 1971

Ireland, Kenneth

1 The Fogou 1977
2 The cove 1979
3 The quail message 1980

Iseborg, Harry

1 John and the red parrot 1964
2 John's day at sea 1968

3 John and the big dog 1976
4 John sails his boat 1977
□
1 Paul, Sally and the fox cub 1968
2 Paul, Sally and the wash-tub 1969
3 Paul, Sally and Little Grey 1970
4 Paul and Sally at Christmas 1976

Iwasaki, C.
1 Momoko's lovely day 1969
2 A brother for Momoko 1970
3 Momoko and the pretty bird 1972
4 Momoko's birthday 1973

Jackson, R. E.
1 The poltergeist 1968
2 Aunt Eleanor 1969
3 The witch of Castle Kerry 1968
4 Street of Mars 1971
5 The wheel of the Finfolk
Chronological order, 1 is about the father of Hamish and Mollie MacGillan.

Jacques, Faith
1 Tilly's house 1979
2 Tilly's rescue 1981

Janosch
1 The trip to Panama 1978
2 The treasure-hunting trip 1980
3 A letter for tiger 1981

Jansson, Tove
MOOMIN SERIES:
1 Finn Family Moomintroll 1950
2 Comet in Moominland 1951
3 Exploits of Moominpappa 1952
4 Moomin, Mymble and little My 1953
5 Moomin-summer madness 1955
6 Moominland midwinter 1958
7 Tales from Moominvalley 1963
8 Moominpappa at sea 1966
9 Moominvalley in November 1971
2 was published two years before 1 in Finland and is logically the one to be read first.

Jellinek, Joanna
1 Georgina and the dragon 1977
2 Raviola sneezes 1980

Jezard, Alison
1 Albert 1967
2 Albert in Scotland 1969
3 Albert and Henry 1970
4 Albert's Christmas 1971
5 Albert up the river 1971
6 Albert and digger 1972
7 Albert and tum tum 1973
8 Albert goes to sea 1973
9 Albert police bear 1975
10 Albert goes trekking 1976
11 Albert's circus 1977
12 Albert goes treasure hunting 1978
13 Albert on the farm 1979

Joanny, A.
1 Nim and his world 1972
2 Nim and his money 1973
3 Nim and his food 1974
4 Nim buys and sells 1974

Johns, Capt. William Earl
REX CLINTON SERIES:
1 Kings of space 1954
2 Return to Mars 1955
3 Now to the stars 1954
4 To outer space 1957
5 The edge of beyond 1958
6 The death rays of Ardilla 1959
7 To worlds unknown 1960
8 Quest for the perfect planet 1961
9 Worlds of wonder: more adventures in space 1962
10 Man who vanished into space 1963
□
1 Adventure bound 1955
2 Adventure unlimited 1957
□
1 King of the Commandos 1943
2 Gimlet goes again 1944
3 Gimlet comes home 1946
4 Gimlet mops up 1947
5 Gimlet's oriental quest 1948
6 Gimlet lends a hand 1949
7 Gimlet bores in 1950
8 Gimlet off the map 1951
9 Gimlet gets the answer 1952
10 Gimlet takes a job 1954
□
1 Worrals of the W.A.A.F. 1941
2 Worrals carries on 1942
3 Worrals flies again 1942

4 Worrals on the warpath 1943
5 Worrals goes East 1944
6 Worrals of the islands 1945
7 Worrals in the wilds 1947
8 Worrals down under 1948
9 Worrals goes afoot 1949
10 Worrals in the wastelands 1949
11 Worrals investigates 1950

'Comrades in arms' contains stories of 'Biggles', 'Worrals' and 'Gimlet'.

□

BIGGLES SERIES:

1 The Camels are coming 1932
2 The cruise of the Condor 1933
3 Biggles of the Camel Squadron 1934
4 Biggles flies again 1934
5 Biggles learns to fly 1935
6 The black peril 1935
7 Biggles flies East 1935
8 Biggles hits the trail 1935
9 Biggles in France 1935
10 Biggles and Co. 1936
11 Biggles in Africa 1936
12 Biggles – Air Commodore 1937
13 Biggles flies West 1937
14 Biggles flies South 1938
15 Biggles goes to war 1938
16 The Biggles Omnibus 1938
17 The rescue flight 1939
18 Biggles in Spain 1939
19 Biggles flies North 1939
20 Biggles – secret agent 1940
21 The Biggles flying omnibus 1940
22 Biggles in the Baltic 1940
23 Biggles in the South Seas 1940
24 Biggles defies the Swastika 1941
25 Biggles sees it through 1941
26 Spitfire parade 1941
27 The third Biggles omnibus 1941
28 Biggles in the jungle 1942
29 Biggles sweeps the desert 1942
30 Biggles – charter pilot 1943
31 Biggles in Borneo 1943
32 Biggles 'Fails to return' 1943
33 Biggles in the Orient 1945
34 Biggles delivers the goods 1946
35 Sergeant Bigglesworth CID 1947
36 Biggles' second case 1948
37 Biggles hunts big game 1948
38 Biggles takes a holiday 1948
39 Biggles breaks the silence 1949
40 Biggles gets his men 1950
41 Another job for Biggles 1951
42 Biggles goes to school 1951
43 Biggles works it out 1952
44 Biggles takes the case 1952
45 Biggles follows on 1952
46 Biggles – air detective 1952
47 Biggles and the Black Raider 1953
48 Biggles in the Blue 1953
49 The first Biggles omnibus 1953
50 Biggles in the Gobi 1953
51 Biggles of the Special Air Police 1953
52 Biggles cuts it fine 1954
53 Biggles and the pirate treasure 1954
54 Biggles Foreign Legionnaire 1954
55 Biggles pioneer airfighter 1954
56 Biggles in Australia 1955
57 Biggles' Chinese puzzle 1955
58 Biggles of 266 1955
59 Biggles Air Detective omnibus 1956
60 No rest for Biggles 1956
61 Biggles takes charge 1956
62 Biggles makes ends meet 1957
63 Biggles of the Interpol 1957
64 Biggles on the Home Front 1957
65 Biggles presses on 1958
66 Biggles on mystery island 1958
67 Biggles buries the hatchet 1958
68 Biggles in Mexico 1959
69 Biggles' combined operation 1959
70 Biggles at the World's End 1959
71 Biggles and the Leopards of Zinn 1960
72 Biggles goes home 1960
73 Biggles and the poor rich boy 1960
74 Biggles forms a syndicate 1961
75 Biggles and the missing millionaire 1961
76 Biggles goes alone 1962
77 Orchids for Biggles 1962
78 Biggles sets a trap 1962
79 Biggles takes it rough 1963
80 Biggles takes a hand 1963
81 Biggles' special case 1963
82 Biggles and the plane that disappeared 1963
83 Biggles flies to work 1963
84 Biggles and the lost sovereigns 1964
85 Biggles and the Black Mask 1964
86 Biggles investigates 1964
87 Biggles looks back 1965
88 Biggles and the plot that failed 1965
89 Biggles and the blue moon 1965
90 Biggles adventure omnibus 1965

91 Biggles scores a bull 1965
92 Biggles in the Terai 1966
93 Biggles and the gun runners 1966
94 Biggles sorts it out 1967
95 Biggles and the dark intruder 1967
96 Biggles and the penitent thief 1967
97 Biggles and the deep blue sea 1967
98 The Boy Biggles 1968
99 Biggles and the Underworld 1968
100 Biggles and the Little Green God 1969
101 Biggles and the noble lord 1969
102 Biggles sees too much 1970

Johnston, Tony
1 The adventures of Mole and Troll 1975
2 Mole and Troll trim the tree 1976
3 Night noises and other Mole and Troll stories

Jones, Harold
1 There and back again
2 Silver bells and cockle-shells; A Bunby adventure 1979

Jones, Olive
JENNY AND SIMON:
1 Summer in Barfield 1968
2 Pets in Barfield 1968
3 Adventure in Barfield 1971
4 Jenny lives in Barfield 1971

Jones, Peter
TALES OF TERRY TROTTER:
1 Wheldon the weed 1961
2 Crump the crock 1962
3 Wheldon the wizard 1963
4 Mathematics or blood 1964

Kastner, Erich
1 Emil and the detectives 1930
2 Emil and the three twins 1935
3 The 35th of May 1933

Kaufmann, Herbert
CAPTAIN GEVER:
1 The lost Sahara trail 1960
2 The city under the desert sands 1965

Kavanagh, Patrick Joseph
1 Scarf Jack 1978
2 Rebel for good 1980

Kay, Mara
1 Mahsa 1968
2 The youngest lady in waiting 1969

Keats, Ezra Jack
PETER SERIES:
1 The snowy day 1967
2 Whistle for Willie 1966
3 Peter's chair 1968
4 A letter to Amy 1969
5 Goggles 1970
6 Hi cat! 1971
7 Pet show 1972

Keene, Carolyn
NANCY DREW SERIES:
1 The secret of the old clock 1954
2 The hidden staircase 1954
3 The bungalow mystery 1954
4 The mystery at Lilac Inn 1954
5 The secret at Shadow Ranch 1954
6 The secret of Red Gate farm 1954
7 The clue in the diary 1960
8 Nancy's mysterious letter 1960
9 The sign of the twisted candles 1960
10 The password to Larkspur Lane 1960
11 The clue of the broken locket 1963
12 The message in the hollow oak 1963
13 Mystery of the ivory charm
14 The whispering statue
15 The haunted bridge
16 Clue of the tapping heels
17 Mystery of the brass-bound trunk
18 Mystery of the moss-covered mansion
19 Quest of the missing map
20 The clue in the jewel box
21 The secret in the old attic
22 Clue in the crumbling wall
23 Mystery of the toiling bell
24 The clue in the old album 1967
25 The ghost of Blackwood Hall 1967
26 The clue of the leaning chimney 1966
27 The secret of the wooden lady 1966
28 The clue of the black eyes 1966
29 The mystery at the ski jump 1967
30 The clue of the velvet mask 1965
31 Mystery of the fire dragon 1963
32 The clue of the dancing puppet
33 The hidden window mystery 1964
34 The haunted showboat 1964
35 The moonstone castle mystery 1964
36 The clue of the whistling bagpipes 1964

37 The secret of the golden pavilion 1963
38 The clue in the old stage coach
39 The ringmaster's secret 1965
40 The scarlet slipper mystery 1965
41 The witchtree symbol 1965
42 Phantom of Pine Hill 1966
43 The spider sapphire mystery
44 Mystery of the 99 steps 1967
45 The invisible intruder
46 The clue in the crossword cypher 1968
47 The double jinx mystery
48 The secret of the forgotten city
49 The secret of Mirror Bay
50 Mystery of Crocodile Island
51 Mystery of the Glowing Eye
52 The strange message in the parchment
53 The crooked bannister
54 The mysterious mannequin
55 The sky phantom
56 The thirteenth pearl
56 The flying saucer mystery
58 The triple hoax
59 The secret of the Swiss chalet
60 The secret in the old lace 1981
61 Greek symbol mystery
62 The Kachina doll mystery 1982
63 Twin dilemma
64 Swami's ring
Many republished in paperback. 'The Nancy Drew Sleuth Book' 1979.

DANA GIRLS SERIES:
1 By the light of the study lamp
2 The secret at Lone Tree cottage
3 In the shadow of the tower
4 A three-cornered mystery
5 The mystery of the stone tiger
6 The riddle of the frozen fountain

Keeping, Charles *(Illus.), see* **Garfield L.** *and* **Bushen, E.**

Keith, Shona
1 Harry goes to a fancy-dress 1979
2 Harry's baggy jumper 1979
3 Harry's new hobby 1979

Kellog, Steven
1 Pinkerton behave 1981
2 A rose for Pinkerton 1982
3 Tallyho Pinkerton 1983

Kemp, Gene
1 The prime of Tamworth pig 1972
2 Tamworth pig saves the trees 1973
3 Tamworth pig and the litter 1975
4 Christmas with Tamworth pig 1977
□
1 The turbulent term of Tyke Tiler 1977
2 Gowie Corby plays chicken 1979
Both stories are set in the same school but are not actually sequels.

Kendall, Carol
1 The Minnipins 1965
2 The whisper of Glocken 1967

Kent, Margaret
FOUR SEASONS AT CHERRY-TREE FARM:
1 Spring at Cherry-Tree Farm 1942
2 Summer at Cherry-Tree Farm 1942
3 Autumn at Cherry-Tree Farm 1942
4 Winter at Cherry-Tree Farm 1943
□
1 The twins at Hillside Farm 1942
2 The twins at home 1947
3 The twins at the seaside 1943
4 The twins and the move 1962

Kerr, Judith
1 When Hitler stole pink rabbit 1971
2 The other way round 1975
3 A small person far away 1978
Stories of a Jewish girl during World War II and afterwards.
□
1 Mog the forgetful cat 1970
2 Mog's Christmas 1976
3 Mog and the baby 1980
4 Mog in the dark 1983

Kershaw, John
1 Sally and Jake and a tortoise 1974
2 Sally and Jake go to the fair 1974
3 Sally and Jake on the farm 1974
4 Sally and Jake play bowls 1974

Kimenye, Barbara
MOSES SERIES:
1 Moses
2 Moses and Mildred 1967
3 Moses and the kidnappers 1968
4 Moses in trouble 1968
5 Moses in a muddle 1970

6 Moses and the ghost 1971
7 Moses on the move 1972
8 Moses and the penpal 1973
9 Moses the camper 1973

King, Kay

1 The life and times of Cornelius Plum 1972
2 Six days in the life of Cornelius Plum 1974

Kingston, William Henry Giles

1 Three midshipmen 1862
2 Three lieutenants 1874
3 Three commanders 1875
4 Three admirals 1877

Kirk, Thomas Hobson

WILLIAM AND SUSAN:
1 Back to the wall 1967
2 The river gang 1968
3 The Ardrey ambush 1969

Kleberger, Ilse

1 Grandmother Oma 1968
2 Grandmother Oma and the green caravan 1969

Knight, Frank

CHICHESTER HARBOUR SERIES:
1 Mudlarks and mysteries 1955
2 Family on the tide 1956
3 Please keep off the mud 1957
4 Shadows in the mud 1960

Knight, Peter

1 Gold of the snow goose 1961
2 Assassin's castle 1962
ANTHONY DAINTREY SERIES:
1 Bramble fortress 1962
2 The Boreas adventure 1963

Knox, Thomas Wallace

1 The boy travellers in the Far East. Part 1. Adventures of two youths in a journey to Japan and China 1879
2 The boy travellers in the Far East. Part 2. Adventures of two youths in a journey to Siam and Java 1880
3 The boy travellers in Ceylon and India
4 The boy travellers in the Far East. Part 4. Adventures of two youths in a journey to Egypt and the Holy Land 1883
5 The boy travellers in the Russian Empire 1886
6 The boy travellers in Africa
7 The boy travellers in South America 1886
8 The boy travellers in the Congo 1887
9 The boy travellers in Australasia 1889
10 The boy travellers in Mexico 1889
11 The boy travellers in Great Britain and Ireland 1890
12 The boy travellers in Northern Europe 1891
13 The boy travellers in Central Europe 1889
14 The boy travellers in the Levant 1895
15 The boy travellers in Southern Europe 1893

This once famous series was based on the author's own travels as a newspaper correspondent.

Kraus, Robert

1 Pinchpenny Mouse 1976
2 The gondolier of Venice 1977

Kruse, Max

1 The Urmal from the Ice Age 1973
2 The Urmal in space 1973

Krüss, James

1 Florentine 1967
2 Florentine on holiday 1967

Kuratomi, Chizuko

1 Remember Mister Bear 1967
2 Mister Bear goes to sea 1968
3 Mister Bear in the air 1969
4 Mister Bear's trumpet 1970
5 Mister Bear and the robbers 1971
6 Mister Bear, station master 1972
7 Mister Bear and apple jam 1973
8 Mister Bear's Christmas 1974
9 Mister Bear's drawing 1975
10 Mister Bear, babyminder 1976
11 Mister Bear's meal 1978
12 Mister Bear postman 1979
13 Mister Bear's shadow 1980
14 Mister Bear, baker 1981
15 Mister Bear's winter sleep 1982

Kyle, Elisabeth, *pseud.* **[Agnes Mary Robertson Dunlop]**
FURZE SERIES:
1 Visitors from England 1941
2 Vanishing island 1942
3 The seven sapphires 1944
4 Holly hotel 1945
5 West wind 1948
6 House on the hill 1949

Lang, Andrew
1 Prince Prigio 1889
2 Prince Ricardo of Pantouflia 1893
3 Tales of a fairy court 1906

Langholm, A. D.
CLOVER CLUB SERIES:
1 The Clover Club and the house of mystery 1978
2 The Clover Club and the adventure that fell out of the sky 1980

Langton, Jane
THE HALL FAMILY SERIES:
1 The diamond in the window 1969
2 Swing in the summerhouse 1970

Larrabeiti, Michael de
1 The Borribles 1976
2 The Borribles go for broke 1982

Lattimore, Eleanor Frances
1 Little Pear 1947
2 Little Pear and his friends
3 Little Pear and the rabbits 1963
4 More about Little Pear

Lauber, Patricia
1 Clarence and the burglar
2 Clarence and the cat 1979

Lavelle, Sheila
1 My best fiend 1980
2 The fiend next door 1982
□
1 Ursula Bear 1977
2 Ursula dancing 1979
3 Ursula exploring 1980
4 Ursula flying 1981

Lawrence, Ann
1 The travels of Oggy 1973
2 Oggy at home 1977
3 Oggy and the holiday 1979

Lea, Alec
1 To sunset and beyond 1970
2 Beth Varden at sunset 1977

Leach, Christopher
DAVE BOURNE SERIES:
1 Tomorrow in Atlantis 1972
2 A temporary open air life 1973
3 Searching for skylights 1976

Leavy, Una
1 Shoes for Tom 1981
2 Tom's garden 1981

Lebrun, Claude *and* **Bour, Daniele**
1 Little Brown Bear's walk 1982
2 Little Brown Bear's story 1982
3 Little Brown Bear's tricycle 1982
4 Little Brown Bear's cold 1982
5 Little Brown Bear won't eat 1982
6 Little Brown Bear is cross 1982
7 Little Brown Bear's bad day
8 Little Brown Bear's playtime
9 Little Brown Bear's birthday egg
10 Little Brown Bear's snowball
11 Little Brown Bear can cook
12 Little Brown Bear is big!

Lee, Benjamin
MIKE AND BILL:
1 Paganini strikes again 1971
2 The man in fifteen 1972

Lee, Robert
1 Fishy business 1981
2 Microfish 1983

Lee, Samantha
OWEN LIGHTBRINGER, SON OF THE SUN, TRILOGY:
1 The quest for the sword of Infinity 1979
2 The land where serpents rule 1980
3 The path through the circle of time 1980

Leeson, Robert

THE MORTENS:

1 Maroon boy 1974
2 Bess 1975
3 The white horse 1977

GRANGE HILL:

1 Grange Hill
2 Grange Hill goes wild 1980
3 Grange Hill for sale 1981
4 Grange Hill rules O.K.
5 Grange Hill home and away 1982

Stories based on characters created by Phil Redmund for the BBC TV series.

□

1 40 days of Tucker J 1983
2 Tucker's luck 1983

1 features one of the characters from the early stories of Grange Hill.

See also **Redmond, Phil**

Le Feuvre, Amy

SCRATCH:

1 Scratch and Co. 1969
2 The hunting of Wilberforce Pike 1970

2 precedes 1 in time.

Le Guin, Ursula

EARTHSEA TRILOGY

1 A wizard of Earthsea 1971
2 The tombs of Atuan 1972
3 The farthest shore 1973

Also available in one volume, 'Earthsea' 1977.

Leigh, Roberta

1 The adventures of Mr Hero 1961
2 Mr Hero and the Raggler children 1961

□

1 Sara and Hoppity 1960
2 Sara and Hoppity make new friends 1960
3 Sara and Hoppity get lost 1961
4 Sara and Hoppity find a cat 1961

□

1 Tomahawk 1960
2 Tomahawk and the river of gold 1960
3 Tomahawk and the tomb of White Moose 1961
4 Tomahawk and the animals of the wild 1961

□

1 Torchy in Topsy Turvy Land 1960
2 Torchy and Bossy Boots 1962
3 Torchy and his two best friends 1962
4 Torchy and the magic beam 1960
5 Torchy and the twinkling star 1962

Leitch, Patricia

JINNY SERIES:

1 For love of a horse 1979
2 A devil to ride 1980
3 The summer riders 1980
4 Night of the Red Horse
5 Gallop to the hills
6 Horse in a million 1980
7 Magic pony 1982
8 Ride like the wind

L'Engle, Madeline

1 Meet the Austins 1966
2 The Young Unicorns 1969

□

1 A wrinkle in time 1963
2 A wind in the door 1975
3 A swiftly tilting planet 1983

Lengstrand, Rolf *and* Rolén, Pierre Louis

1 The long pony race 1965
2 The pony club through smoke and fire 1966

Letts, B., *see* **Doctor Who series**

Lewin, Hugh

1 Jafta 1981
2 Jafta—my father 1981
3 Jafta—my mother 1981
4 Jafta—the wedding 1981
5 Jafta—the journey 1982
6 Jafta—the town 1983

Lewis, Clive Staples

NARNIA SERIES:

1 The lion, the witch and the wardrobe 1950
2 Prince Caspian: The return to Narnia 1951
3 The voyage of the Dawn Treader 1952
4 The silver chair 1953
5 The Horse and his boy 1954

6 The magician's nephew 1955
7 The last battle 1956
The chronological sequence of events is 6, 1, 5, 2, 3, 4, 7. 6 explains the creation of Narnia and explains how ordinary children entered the land. 5 involves purely Narnian characters and takes place during the time when Peter, Susan, Edmund and Lucy are rulers in Narnia.

Lewis, Lorna
1 Shirley goes travelling 1960
2 Shirley goes to America 1961

Lexau, J. M.
1 I should have stayed in bed 1968
2 The rooftop mystery 1969

Lindgren, Astrid Anna Emilia
1 Kati in Italy 1962
2 Kati in America 1963
3 Kati in Paris 1961
□
1 Karlson on the roof 1975
2 Karlson flies again 1977
3 The world's best Karlson 1979
□
1 Emil in the soup tureen 1970
2 Emil's pranks 1973
3 Emil and his clever pig 1975
4 Emil and the bad tooth 1976
5 That Emil 1979
□
1 The six Bullerby children 1961
2 Christmas at Bullerby 1962
3 Cherry time at Bullerby 1964
4 Happy days at Bullerby 1965
5 Springtime in Bullerby 1980
'All about the Bullerby Children' 1970 is an omnibus volume containing 1-4.

1 Pippi Longstocking 1950
2 Pippi goes abroad 1956
3 Pippi in the South Seas 1957
□
1 The mischievous Martens 1968
2 Lotta's bike 1973
3 Lotta's Christmas surprise 1978
4 Lotta leaves home 1978
'Lotta' 1982 combines 'Lotta leaves home' and 'The mischievous Martens'.
□
1 Mardie 1979
2 Mardie to the rescue 1981

Lindgren, B.
1 Sam's ball 1983
2 Sam's bath 1983
3 Bad Sam 1983

Lindsay, Frances
1 Mr Bits and Pieces
2 Bits and Pieces solves a mystery 1978

Lingard, Joan
SADIE AND KEVIN:
1 The twelfth day of July 1970
2 Across the barricades 1972
3 Into exile 1973
4 A proper place 1975
5 Hostages to fortune 1976
MAGGIE MCKINLEY:
1 The clearance 1974
2 The resettling 1975
3 The pilgrimage 1976
4 The reunion 1977
Nos 1-3 also available in an omnibus volume, 'Maggie' 1982.

Little, Sylvia
1 Castle school gets going 1947
2 The twins at Castle school 1947
3 Castle school on holiday 1948
4 Blood royal at Castle school 1949
5 Castle school on the screen 1949
6 Castle school at the cross-roads 1950
7 Castle school on the warpath 1950
8 Castle school in the news 1950

Lively, Penelope
1 Fanny's sister 1977
2 Fanny and the monsters 1979
3 Fanny and the Battle of Potter's piece 1980

Livingstone, M. *and* **Sheridan, John**
1 Eric the wild car 1978
2 Eric and the mad inventor 1978
3 Eric and the lost planes 1978

Lloyd, Errol
1 Nini at carnival 1978
2 Nini on time 1981

Lobel, Arnold

1 Days with Frog and Toad 1970
2 Frog and Toad are friends 1971
3 Frog and Toad together 1973
4 Frog and Toad all year 1977
5 Tales of Frog and Toad
'Frog and Toad tales' 1981 is an omnibus volume containing 1, 2 and 3.

□

1 Mouse tales 1973
2 Mouse soup 1978

Lofgren, Ulf

1 Albin is never afraid 1975
2 Albin lends a hand 1975
3 Albin and the crazy bicycle 1977
4 Albin and the strange umbrella 1977

□

1 Patrick's aeroplane 1974
2 Patrick's circus 1974
3 Patrick's workshop 1975

Lofting, Hugh

1 The story of Dr Dolittle 1920
2 The voyages of Dr Dolittle 1923
3 Dr Dolittle's post office 1924
4 Dr Dolittle's circus 1925
5 Dr Dolittle's zoo 1926
6 Dr Dolittle's caravan 1927
7 Dr Dolittle's garden 1928
8 Dr Dolittle in the moon 1929
9 Dr Dolittle's return 1933
10 Dr Dolittle and the secret lake 1949
11 Dr Dolittle and the green canary 1951
12 Dr Dolittle's Puddlebury adventure 1953
Though not part of the series, Gub Gub is a character in all the volumes, and 'Gub Gub's book' is a separate volume. 'Dr Dolittle and his friends' 1968 is a picture book based on the film 'Dr Dolittle: a treasury' 1968 is an anthology. 'Dr Dolittle and the pirates' by Al Perkins 1968 and 'Travels of Dr Dolittle' 1968 are easy reading stories featuring the characters created by Hugh Lofting.

□

1 The story of Mrs Tubbs 1923
2 Tommy, Tilly and Mrs Tubbs 1937

Lundgren, Ester Ringer-

1 Little Trulsa 1965
2 Little Trulsa's tea party 1966
3 Little Trulsa's secret 1967
4 Little Trulsa's birthday 1968

Lunt, Alice

1 Jeannette's first term 1967
2 Jeannette in the summer term

□

1 Eileen at Redstone Farm 1969
2 Mystery at Redstone Farm 1970

Lydecker, John, *see* **Doctor Who series**

Lynch, Patricia Nora

BROGEEN THE LEPRECHAUN SERIES:

1 Brogeen of the stepping stones 1947
2 Brogeen follows the magic tune 1952
3 Brogeen and the green shoes 1953
4 Brogeen and the bronze lizard 1954
5 Brogeen and the Princess of Sheen 1955
6 Brogeen and the lost castle 1956
7 Brogeen and the black enchanter 1958
8 The stone house at Kilgobbin 1959
9 The longest way round 1961
10 Brogeen and the little wind 1962
11 Brogeen and the red fez 1963
12 Guests at the beech tree 1964

THE TURF CUTTER'S DONKEY SERIES:

1 The turf cutter's donkey 1934
2 The turf cutter's donkey goes visiting 1935
3 The turf cutter's donkey kicks up his heels 1949

Lyon, Elinor

IAN, SOVRA AND CATHIE:

1 The house in hiding 1950
2 We daren't go a-hunting 1951
3 Run-away home 1953
4 Cathie goes wild
5 Daughters of Aradale 1957
6 Carver's journey 1962
7 The dream hunters 1966
8 Strangers at the door 1967

□

1 The day that got lost 1969
2 The wishing pool 1970

MEREDITH FAMILY;

1 Green grow the rushes 1964
2 Echo valley 1965

Macarthur, Wilson

LARRY PEARSON SERIES:

1 Zambezi adventure 1960
2 The valley of hidden gold 1961
3 Guns for the Congo 1963

McBratney, Sam

1 The final correction
2 From the Thorenson Dykes 1980

McCann, Sean

DOVE END FOOTBALL CLUB (GEORGIE GOOD):

1 Goals for glory 1974
2 We are the champions 1975
3 The golden goal 1977
4 Shoot on sight 1981
5 Shooting stars 1978
6 Hot shot 1979
7 The team that nobody wanted 1982

McLean, Allan Campbell

1 Ribbon of fire 1966
2 A sound of trumpets 1967

MacCloskey, Robert

1 Blueberries for Sal 1948
2 One morning in Maine 1967

MacDonald, Betty

1 Mrs Piggle-Wiggle 1947
2 Mrs Piggle-Wiggle's magic 1949
3 Mrs Piggle-Wiggle's farm 1954
4 Hello, Mrs Piggle-Wiggle 1957

MacDonald, Elizabeth

1 The incredible magic plant 1977
2 The little weather house 1978

Macdonald Shelagh

PETHI AND TIMI:

1 A circle of stones 1973
2 Five for me, five for you 1974

Mace, Elizabeth

1 Ransome revisited 1975
2 The travelling man 1976

Stories relating to books by Arthur Ransome.

See also **Ransome, Arthur**

MacGibbon, Jean

1 The great-great rescuers 1967
2 The tall ship 1967

MOLLY AND LIZ:

1 The view finder 1963
2 Liz 1966

MacGinley, Phyllis

1 The horse who lived upstairs 1945
2 The horse who had his picture in the paper 1951

MacGregor, Ellen

1 Miss Pickerell goes to Mars 1957
2 Miss Pickerell and the geiger counter 1958
3 Miss Pickerell goes undersea 1959
4 Miss Pickerell goes to the Arctic 1960

McKee, David

1 Elmer, the story of a patchwork elephant 1968
2 Elmer again and again 1975

□

1 Mr Benn, Red Knight 1967
2 123456789 Benn 1970
3 Big game Benn 1979
4 Big-top Benn 1980

□

1 The magician who lost his magic 1970
2 The magician and the sorcerer 1974
3 The magician and the petnapping 1976
4 The magician and the balloon 1977
5 The magician and the dragon 1979
6 The magician and double trouble 1981

□

1 King Rollo and the new shoes 1979
2 King Rollo and the birthday 1979
3 King Rollo and the bread 1979
4 King Rollo and the dishes 1980
5 King Rollo and the balloons 1980
6 King Rollo and the tree 1980
7 King Rollo and the bath 1981
8 King Rollo and King Frank 1981
9 King Rollo and the search 1981
10 King Rollo's playroom and other stories 1983

See also **Baumann, K.**

MacKenzie, K.

1 The Starke sisters 1963
2 Charlotte 1964
3 Kelford dig 1966

McKimmie, Christopher

1 The shape I'm in 1979
2 The magic day 1979
3 The caught bird 1979
4 One rainy day 1979

McLachlan, Edward

1 Simon in the land of chalk drawings 1970
2 Simon and the chalk drawing army 1971
3 Simon and the moon rocket 1972
4 Simon and the dinosaur 1973

McNaughton, Colin

1 Football crazy 1982
2 Bear crazy 1983

MacNeill, Janet

1 My friend Specs McCann 1957
2 Specs fortissimo 1958
3 Various specs 1961
'Best Specs' 1970 is an omnibus volume.
□
1 The battle of St George without 1968
2 Goodbye, Dove Square 1969

MacNell, James

1 Captain Mettle, V.C. 1955
2 Mettle dives deep 1956
3 Mettle at Woomera 1957

MacVicar, Angus

JEREMY GRANT AND DR MCKINNON SERIES:
1 Lost planet 1957
2 Return to the lost planet 1954
3 Secret of the lost planet 1955
4 Red fire on the lost planet 1959
5 Peril on the lost planet 1960
6 Space agent and the lost planet 1961
7 Space agent and the isles of fire 1962
8 Space agent and the ancient peril 1964
□
1 Super Nova and the rogue satellite 1969
2 Super Nova and the frozen man 1970

Maddock, Reginald Bertram

1 Corrigan and the black riders 1957
2 Corrigan and the Tomb of Opi 1957
3 Corrigan and the white cobra 1958
4 Corrigan and the yellow peril 1958
5 Corrigan and the dream makers 1959
6 Corrigan and the golden pagoda 1959
7 Corrigan and the blue crater 1960
8 Corrigan and the red lions 1962
9 Corrigan and the green tiger 1961
10 Corrigan and the little people 1963
□
1 Rocky and the lions 1957
2 Rocky and the elephant 1962

Maguire, Michael

1 Mylor: the most powerful horse in the world 1977
2 Mylor the kidnap 1978

Main, C.

MERRILL AND ALEX:
1 White planet
2 Planet of evil 1983

Makhanlall, David

1 The best of Brer Anansi 1973
2 The invincible Brer Anansi 1974
3 Brer Anansi strikes again 1976
4 Brer Anansi's bag of tricks 1978
5 Love live Brer Anansi 1979
6 The further adventures of Brer Anansi 1980

Mamlok, Gwyneth

1 Candy and Peppermint 1965
2 Candy and the rocking horse 1965
3 Candy in the Tower 1966
4 Candy and the pony 1966
5 Candy and Ginger 1966
6 Candy and the golden eagle 1966

Manning, Rosemary

1 Greensmoke 1957
2 Dragon in danger 1959
3 The dragon's quest 1961
4 Dragon in the harbour 1980

Mantle, Winifred

1 Jonnesty 1974
2 Jonnesty in winter 1975

Margolis, Richard J.
1 Wish again Big Bear
2 Big Bear to the rescue 1977

Mariana, *pseud.*
1 Miss Flora McFlimsey and little laughing water 1970
2 Miss Flora McFlimsey's birthday 1970
3 Miss Flora McFlimsey's Christmas Eve 1970
4 Miss Flora McFlimsey's Easter bonnet 1970
5 Miss Flora McFlimsey and the baby new year 1970
6 Miss Flora McFlimsey, Queen of the May 1972

Marino, Dorothy
1 Buzzy Bear goes south 1964
2 Buzzy Bear goes camping 1965
3 Buzzy Bear and the rainbow 1968
4 Buzzy Bear's first day at school 1971

Marks, James MacDonald
1 Jason 1973
2 The triangle 1974

Marshall, James
1 George and Martha one fine day 1981
2 George and Martha rise and shine 1982

Marter, Ian, *see* **Doctor Who series**

Martin, John Percival
1 Uncle 1964
2 Uncle cleans up 1965
3 Uncle and his detective 1966
4 Uncle and the treacle trouble 1967
5 Uncle and Claudius the camel 1969
6 Uncle and the battle for Badgertown 1973

Martin, Nancy
1 Call the vet 1955
2 Vet, in the making 1957
JEAN SERIES:
1 Jean behind the counter 1963
2 Jean, teenage fashion buyer 1964
□
1 Young farmers at Gaythorne 1954
2 Young farmers in Denmark 1955
3 Young farmers in Scotland 1956
□
1 Call the nurse 1966
2 Call the courier 1967
□
1 Teresa joins the Red Cross 1969
2 Red Cross challenge 1970

Martin, Robert, *pseud.* **[Reginald Alex Martin]**
1 Joey of Jasmine Street 1954
2 Joey and the river pirates 1954
3 Joey and the mail robbers 1955
4 Joey and the Blackbird Gang 1956
5 Joey and the helicopter 1956
6 Joey and the square of gold 1957
7 Joey and the magic eye 1956
8 Joey and the city ghosts 1957
9 Joey and the Royalist treasure 1957
10 Joey and the squib 1958
11 Joey and the smuggler's legend 1958
12 Joey: soap box driver 1958
13 Joey and the magic pony 1959
14 Joey and the secret engine 1960
15 Joey and the master plan 1961
16 Joey and the detectives 1962
17 Joey and the magician 1963
18 Joey and the pickpocket 1964
19 Joey and the trainrobbers 1965
□
1 Tony and the champ 1963
2 Tony and the secret money 1964
□
1 The gold elephant 1959
2 The money mystery 1960
3 The secret boat 1961
DANCE AND CO. DETECTIVES:
1 The mystery of the T.V. crooks 1960
2 The mystery of the poisoned puppet 1962
3 The mystery of the motorway 1961
4 The mystery of the friendly forger 1958
5 The mystery of the golden skulls 1959
6 The mystery of the long shadow 1958
7 The mystery of the bullion robbery 1960
8 Mystery of the car bandits 1958
9 Mystery of the pay-snatchers 1963
10 Mystery of the missing passenger 1964

Masefield, John
1 The midnight folk 1927
2 The box of delights 1935

Mason, Miriam Evangeline
1 Caroline and her kettle named Maud 1966
2 Caroline and the seven little words 1967

Masters, Anthony, *see* **Saunders, Michael**

Matthews, Patrick and Mollie
1 Teddy Edward and the contraption 1975
2 Teddy Edward becomes a Red Indian 1975
3 Teddy Edward's magic music box 1976
4 Teddy Edward's magic journey 1976
5 Snowy Toes and the music box 1976
6 Teddy Edward in Timbuctoo 1976
7 Teddy Edward goes to Mount Everest 1976

Mayer, Mercer
1 Achoo
2 Oops

Mayne, William
CHOIR SERIES:
1 A swarm in May 1955
2 Chorister's cake 1956
3 Cathedral Wednesday 1960
4 Words and music 1963
□
1 Skippy 1972
2 Skippy and the twin planets 1982

Meer, Van Der, Ron and A.
1 My brother Sammy 1978
2 Sammy and Mara 1978
□
1 Basil and Boris in London 1978
2 Basil and Boris in North America 1978

Melinsky, Renate
1 The children of the Crescent 1974
2 The Crescent children on the green 1974

Meyer, Renate
1 Little Nittle and Threadle 1971
2 Mr Knitted and the family tree 1972

Meynell, Laurence, *pseud.* **[A. Stephen Tring]**
1 Smoky Joe 1952
2 Smoky Joe in trouble 1953
3 Smoky Joe goes to school 1956
□
1 Nurse Ross takes over 1959
2 Nurse Ross shows the way 1959
3 Nurse Ross saves the day 1960
4 Nurse Ross and the Doctor 1962
5 Good luck, Nurse Ross 1963
ROBIN WESTON SERIES:
1 Scoop 1964
2 The suspect scientist 1966
3 Shadow in the sun 1966
□
1 Penny dreadful 1949
2 Penny triumphant 1953
3 Penny penitent 1953
4 Penny puzzled 1955
5 Penny dramatic 1956
6 Penny in Italy 1957
7 Penny and the pageant 1959
8 Penny says goodbye 1961
□
1 Barry's exciting year 1951
2 Barry's great day 1954
3 Barry gets his wish 1952
The author used the pseudonym A. S. Tring for his earlier books.

Mikura, Vera Ferra
THE STALISLAUS FAMILY:
1 The voyagers 1966
2 The painters 1970

Miller, Albert G.
1 Fury 1960
2 Fury and the mustangs 1961

Miller, Edna
1 Mousekin's golden house 1966
2 Mousekin finds a friend 1967
3 Mousekin's close call

Miller, Elizabeth *and* **Cohen, Jane**
1 Cat and dog have a contest
2 Cat and dog and the mixed up week
3 Cat and dog give a party
4 Cat and dog raise the roof
5 Cat and dog take a trip

Miller, Margaret Jessy

THE KINGDOM OF CALEDON:

1 The Queen's music 1961
2 The powers of the Sapphire 1962
3 Doctor Boomer 1964

□

1 Mousetails 1967
2 Willow and Albert 1968
3 Willow and Albert are stowaways 1968
4 The big brown teapot 1979
5 The mad muddle 1982

□

1 The fearsome island 1975
2 The fearsome road 1975
3 The fearsome tide 1976

Miller, Moira

1 Oh, Abigail! 1981
2 Just like Abigail! 1983

Mills, Annette

1 Muffin the mule 1949
2 More about Muffin 1950
3 Muffin and the magic hat 1951
4 Here comes Muffin 1952
5 Muffin at the seaside 1953
6 Muffin' splendid adventure 1954

Milne, Alan Alexander

1 Winnie the Pooh 1926
2 The house at Pooh Corner 1928

Winnie the Pooh evolved from Edward Bear in the verse collection 'When we were very young' 1924, and also appears in the verse collection 'Now we are six' 1928. Methuen have also published a series 'Piglet books' taking individual stories from 1 and 2 and presenting them in a suitable format for younger readers. Christopher Milne, the son of the author, describes his childhood in 'Enchanted Places' 1977 and 'The path through the trees'.

Milroy, Clarita

1 A highland quest 1956
2 The secret of the caves 1957

Minarik, Else H.

1 Father bear comes home 1960
2 Little bear's friend 1961
3 Little bear's visit 1962
4 Little bear 1965
5 Kiss for little bear 1969

Omnibus volume published 1982.

Mirsky, Reba Paeff

1 Thirty-one brothers and sisters 1952
2 Seven grandmothers 1955

Stories about a Zulu girl.

Mitchell, Elyne

1 The silver brumby 1958
2 Silver Brumby's daughter 1960
3 Silver Brumbies of the South 1965
4 Silver Brumby kingdom 1966
5 Silver Brumby whirlwind 1973
6 Moon filly 1968
7 Son of Whirlwind 1977
8 The cold from Snowy River 1980
9 Snow River Brumby 1981
10 Brumby racer 1982

Mitson, Angela *and* **Reed, Giles**

1 The Munch Bunch go camping 1980
2 The Munch Bunch at the seaside 1980
3 The Munch Bunch have a party 1980

Moffit, V. M., *see* **Porter, E. H.**

Mogenson, Jan

1 Just before dawn 1982
2 Ted and the Chinese princess 1983

Montgomery, John

1 Foxy 1960
2 My friend Foxy 1961

Montgomery, Lucy Maud

1 Anne of Green Gables 1908
2 Anne of Avonlea 1909
3 Chronicles of Avonlea 1912
4 Anne of the island 1915
5 Anne's house of dreams 1918
6 Rainbow Valley 1919
7 Anne of Windy Willows 1936
8 Anne of Ingleside 1939
9 Further chronicles of Avonlea 1942

'The Road to yesterday' 1975 is a posthumous and recently discovered collection of stories. 'The Wheel of things' by M. Gillen 1976 contains a complete list of all books by L. M. Montgomery and describes her life story.

□

1 The story girl 1911
2 The golden road 1914
□
1 Emily of New Moon 1923
2 Emily climbs 1925
3 Emily's quest 1927
□
1 Pat of Silver Bush 1933
2 Mistress Pat 1935

Montgomery, Rutherford George
1 The capture of the Golden Stallion 1954
2 The Golden Stallion's revenge 1955
3 The Golden Stallion to the rescue 1956
4 The Golden Stallion's victory 1957
5 The Golden Stallion and the wolf dog 1959
6 The Golden Stallion's adventure at Redstone 1960
7 The Golden Stallion and the mysterious feud 1970

Moon, Heather
1 Winklepicker 1981
2 Winklepicker goes South 1982

Moore, Patrick
GRENFELL AND WRIGHT:
1 Master of the Moon 1952
2 The Island of fear 1954
MAURICE GRAY SERIES:
1 Mission to Mars 1955
2 The domes of Mars 1956
3 The voices of Mars 1957
4 Peril on Mars 1958
5 Raiders of Mars 1959
GREGORY QUEST
1 Quest of Spaceways 1955
2 World of mists 1956
ROBIN NORTH AND REX REDMAYNE SERIES:
1 Wanderer in space 1961
2 Crater of fear 1962
3 Invader from space 1963
4 Caverns of the moon 1964

Morecambe, Eric
1 The reluctant vampire 1982
2 The vampire's revenge 1983

Morgan, Alison
1 Fish 1971
2 Pete 1972
3 Ruth Crane 1973
4 At Willie Tucker's place 1975

Morgan, Helen
1 Meet Mary Kate 1965
2 Mary Kate and the jumble bear 1966
3 Mary Kate and the school bus 1970
□
1 Mrs Pinny and the blowing day 1968
2 Mrs Pinny and the sudden snow 1969
3 Mrs Pinny and the salty sea day 1972
□
1 Satchkin Patchkin 1966
2 Mother Farthing's luck 1971

Morris, *joint author, see* **Goscinny** *and* **Morris**

Morris, Johnny
1 Billy Bullrush meets Len the shrew 1974
2 Billy Bullrush and the house martins 1975

Morrison, J. Strang, *pseud.* **[William Albert Strang Thom]**
1 Wind force seven 1958
2 The Monach light 1961

Morrow, C.
1 The singing and the gold
2 The noonday thread

Morton, J.
1 Jimmy and the giant cleaner 1971
2 Jimmy and the rubber boat 1971
3 Jimmy and the ladder 1972
4 Jimmy and the plant food 1972

Moss, Nancy
CLIFF HOUSE SERIES:
1 School on the precipice 1954
2 Susan's stormy term 1955
3 Strange quest at Cliff House 1956
4 The Cliff House monster 1957
5 The riddle of Cliff House 1959

Moss, Robert
1 First challenge book of Brownie stories 1980
2 Second challenge book of Brownie stories 1981

Moss, Roberta
1 Jenny of the Fourth 1953
2 Jenny's exciting term 1954

Muir, Frank
1 What-a-mess 1978
2 What-a-mess the good 1978
3 Prince What-a-mess 1979
4 Super What-a-mess 1980
5 What-a-mess and the cat next door 1981
6 What-a-mess in spring 1982
7 What-a-mess in summer 1982
8 What-a-mess in autumn 1982
9 What-a-mess in winter 1982
10 What-a-mess at the seaside 1983
'What-a-mess and What-a-mess the good' 1979, a combined edition of these two titles. 6-9 are small format picture books.

Muir, Maria
1 Torridon's triumph 1960
2 Torridon's surprise 1961
3 Torridons in Spain 1962
4 Torridons in trouble 1963

Muirden, James
1 Space intruder 1964
2 The moon-winners 1965

Mure, Geoffrey Reginald Gilchrist
1 Josephine 1937
2 The boots and Josephine 1939

Murphy, Jill
1 The worst witch 1975
2 The worst witch strikes again 1979
3 A bad spell for the worst witch 1982

Murray, Lillian
1 Ginnie and the snow gypsies 1958
2 In the track of the huskies 1960

Nakatani, Chiyoko
1 My day on the farm 1976
2 My teddy bear 1976 (pub. 1975 in Japan)
3 My animal friends 1979

Naylor, Phyllis Reynolds
1 Witch water 1979
2 The witch herself 1979

Needham, Violet
1 The black riders 1956
2 The Red Rose of Ruvina 1957

Needle, Jan
1 The size spies 1979
2 Another fine mess 1981

Nesbit, Edith
TREASURE SEEKERS SERIES:
1 The story of the treasure seekers 1899
2 The wouldbegoods 1901
3 The new treasure seekers 1904
4 Oswald Bastable and others 1905
4 is a collection of short stories, four of which concern Oswald Bastable. The Bastable children also appear in 'The Red House', an adult novel. 'The conscience pudding' is from 3, separately published, 1973, for younger children.
□
1 Five children and it 1902
2 The phoenix and the carpet 1904
3 The story of the amulet 1906
'Five children and it and other stories' 1979 contains all three stories.
□
1 The house of Arden 1908
2 Harding's luck 1909

Neville, Malcolm
1 Meet the Sandmen 1973
2 The Sandmen in danger 1974
3 The Sandmen and the smugglers 1977

Newman, Marjorie
1 Wilkins the armchair cat 1977
2 Wilkins gets a job 1980

Newman, Robert
1 Merlin's mistake 1973
2 The testing of Tertius 1974

Niall, Ian
BILLY BOYO AND ALBERT FINN
1 Fishing for trouble 1968
2 The owl hunters 1969

Nicholls, Beverley
JILL AND JUDY SERIES:
1 The tree that sat down 1945
2 The stream that stood still 1948

3 The mountain of magic 1950
4 The wickedest witch in the world 1971

Nickless, W.
ROTHERSIDE SERIES:
1 Owlglass 1965
2 The nitehood 1966
3 Molepie 1967

Nicoll, Helen *and* **Pienkowski, Jan**
1 Meg and Mog 1973
2 Meg at sea 1973
3 Meg's eggs 1973
4 Meg's car 1975
5 Meg's castle 1975
6 Meg's veg 1976
7 Mog's mumps 1976
8 Meg on the moon 1974
9 Mog at the zoo 1982

Norton, Andre, *pseud.* **[Alice Mary Norton]**
1 Steel magic 1967
2 Octagon magic 1968
3 Fur magic 1969
Not sequels but connected.
KRIP VORLAND:
1 Moon of three rings 1969
2 Exiles of the stars 1972
PLANET ARZOR:
1 Catseye 1962
2 The beast master 1966
3 Lord of thunder 1966
□
1 Judgement on Janus 1964
2 Victory on Janus 1967
MURDOC JEM:
1 The Zero Stone 1974
2 Uncharted stars 1974
□
1 The stars are ours 1954
2 Star born 1973
□
1 The sword is drawn 1946
2 Sword in sheath 1953
DANE THORSON:
1 Sargasso of space 1970
2 Plague ship 1971
3 Postmarked the stars 1971
BLAKE WALKER:
1 Crosstime agent 1975
2 The crossroads of time 1976

Norton, Mary
1 The Borrowers 1952
2 The Borrowers afield 1955
3 The Borrowers afloat 1959
4 The Borrowers aloft 1961
5 The Borrowers avenged 1982
Stories of the tiny people who live in human house and are responsible for 'borrowing' the things that get lost. 'Poor Stainless' 1971 is a 'Borrowers' story, but not in the series, written originally as a birthday gift for Eleanor Farjeon. 'Borrowers' omnibus' 1976 contains 1-4.
□
1 The magic bedknob 1945
2 Bonfires and broomsticks 1947
Omnibus edition 'Bedknob and broomstick' 1957.

Oakley, Graham
THE WORTLETHORPE CHRONICLES:
1 The church mouse 1972
2 The church cat abroad 1973
3 The church mice and the moon 1974
4 The church mice spread their wings 1975
5 The church mice adrift 1976
6 The church mice at bay 1978
7 The church mice at Christmas 1980
8 The church mice in action 1982

O'Brien, Edna
1 The dazzle 1981
2 A Christmas treat 1982

O'Dell, Scott
1 Island of the blue dolphins 1961
2 Zia 1977

O'Farrell, Kathleen
THE LATTIMER CHILDREN:
1 Three cheers for Annabelle 1956
2 Off to the sea with Annabelle 1958
3 Cousin Annabelle's Xmas 1959

O'Hara, Mary
1 Flicka (My friend Flicka) 1943
2 Thunderhead, son of Flicka 1945
3 Green grass of Wyoming 1947

Ohlson, Edith Emilie
1 Pippa at Brighton 1937
2 Pippa in Switzerland 1938

3 Pippa at home 1940
4 Pippa and James 1943

Oldfield, Pamela
1 Melanie Brown goes to school 1972
2 Melanie Brown climbs a tree 1973
3 Melanie Brown and the jar of sweets 1974
□
1 The adventures of the Gumby gang 1978
2 The Gumby gang again 1978
3 More about the Gumby gang 1979
4 The Gumby gang on holiday 1980
5 The Gumby gang strikes again 1980
□
1 Katy and Dom 1978
2 Katy and Dom and the last cat 1979
□
1 The Willerbys and the burglar 1981
2 The Willerbys and the haunted mill 1981
3 The Willerbys and the sad clown 1982
4 The Willerbys and the old castle 1982

Oliver, Marjorie Mary
1 Menace on the moor 1960
2 Riddle of the tired pony 1963

Ormerod, Jan
1 Sunshine 1981
2 Moonlight 1982

Osborne, Maureen
1 Here comes the Horribilly 1979
2 Horribilly goes to school 1979

Overton, Jenny
1 The creed country 1967
2 The nightwatch winter 1973

Oxenham, Elsie Jeanette, *pseud.* **[Elsie Jeanette Dunkerley]**
ABBEY GIRLS SERIES:
1 Girls of the Hamlet club 1914
2 The Abbey girls 1920
3 Girls of the Abbey school 1921
4 Abbey girls go back to school 1922
5 The new Abbey girls 1923
6 The Abbey girls again 1924
7 Abbey girls in town 1925
8 Queen of the Abbey girls 1926
9 Jen of the Abbey school 1927
10 The Abbey school 1928
11 The Abbey girls win through 1928
12 The Abbey girls at home 1929
13 Abbey girls on trial 1931
14 Biddy's secret: a romance of the Abbey girls 1932
15 Rosamund's victory 1933
16 Maidlin to the rescue 1934
17 Joy's new adventure 1935
18 Rosamund's tuckshop 1936
19 Maidlin takes the trick 1937
20 Rosamund's castle 1938
21 Maidlin bears the torch 1937
22 Two Joans at the Abbey 1945
23 Schooldays at the Abbey 1938
24 Stowaways at the Abbey 1940
25 Maid of the Abbey 1943
26 An Abbey champion 1946
27 Robins in the Abbey 1947
28 Abbey girls play up 1930
29 A fiddler for the Abbey 1948
30 Secrets of the Abbey 1939
31 Guardians of the Abbey 1950
32 School Jen at the Abbey 1950
33 Rachel in the Abbey 1952
34 Selma at the Abbey 1952
35 Strangers at the Abbey 1953
36 A dancer at the Abbey 1953
37 Song of the Abbey 1955
38 Jandy Mac comes back 1956
39 Tomboys at the Abbey 1957
40 Two queens at the Abbey 1958
This is order of publication, but there are really three series—the original series, a series of 'retrospective' books, and stories of the second generation. See article on the author in 'Junior Bookshelf', Feb. 1966.

Packer, Jo
1 No pony like Pepper 1963
2 Gymkhana trek 1964
3 Pepper leads the string 1965

Paice, Margaret
1 The lucky fall 1959
2 The secrets of Greycliffs 1962
□
1 Colour in the creek 1976
2 Shadow of wings 1979

Palmer, Cyril Everard

1 Beppo Tate and Roy Penner: the runaway marriage brokers
2 The wooing of Beppo Tate 1972

Palmer, Geoffrey *and* Lloyd, Noel

1 Mystery in Sherwood 1962
2 The greenwooders 1963
3 Greenwooders' triumph 1964

Palmer, Juliette

1 Barley sow, barley grow 1979
2 Barley ripe, barley reap 1979
Non fiction books 'Work in a landscape' series.

Palmer, Lynde

HONOUR SERIES:
1 A question of Honour 1893
2 Where Honour leads
MARGARET SERIES:
1 Drifting and steering 1867
2 One day's weaving 1870
3 Archie's shadow
4 John Jack

Pardoe, Margot

1 The ghost boat 1951
2 The boat seekers 1953
3 The Dutch boat 1955
4 The nameless boat 1956
5 The Greek boat mystery 1960

Parish, Peggy

1 Amelia Bedelia 1964
2 Thank you Amelia Bedelia 1965
3 Amelia Bedelia and the surprise shower 1967
4 Come back, Amelia Bedelia 1973
5 Play ball, Amelia Bedelia 1973
6 Good work, Amelia Bedelia 1977
7 Amelia Bedelia and the baby 1982

Park, Ruth

1 The muddle-headed wombat 1963
2 The muddle-headed wombat on holiday 1964
3 The muddle-headed wombat in the treetops 1965
4 The muddle-headed wombat at the school 1966
5 The muddle-headed wombat in the snow 1966
6 The muddle-headed wombat on a rainy day 1970
7 The muddle-headed wombat in the springtime 1970
8 The muddle-headed wombat on the river 1971
9 The muddle-headed wombat on clean-up day 1976
10 The muddle-headed wombat and the invention 1976

Parker, Richard

1 A valley full of pipers 1962
2 Perversity of pipers 1964
3 Beyond the back gate 1977
□
1 The Sunday papers 1976
2 Digging for treasure 1976
3 Sausages on the shore 1976

Parsley, Mary, *ed.*

1 I can choose my bedtime story 1978
2 My second bedtime book of two minute stories 1982

Parsons, Virginia

1 Pinocchio goes on the stage 1977
2 Pinocchio and Geppetto 1977
3 Pinocchio and the money tree 1978
4 Pinocchio plays truant 1978
Picture books taken from Carlo Collodi's original story.

Partridge, Jenny

OAKAPPLE SERIES:
1 Mr Squint 1980
2 Hopfellow 1980
3 Colonel Grunt 1980
4 Peter Pollensnuff 1980
5 Dominia Sly 1981
6 Grandma Snuffles 1981
7 Harriet Plume 1981
8 Lop ear 1981
'Oakapple word treasury' 1982, omnibus edition containing 1-4.

Patchett, Mary Elwyn

1 The Brumby 1958
2 Come home, Brumby 1961
3 The circus Brumby 1963

4 Stranger in the herd 1964
5 The Brumby foal 1965
6 The long ride 1970
7 Rebel Brumby 1972

JEFF JAMES:

1 Warrimoo 1961
2 Dangerous assignment 1962
3 The Venus project 1963

BREVITT SERIES:

1 Undersea treasure hunters 1955
2 Caribbean adventurers 1957
3 The quest of Ati Manu 1960
4 Outback adventure 1957
5 Call of the bush 1959

AJAX SERIES:

1 Ajax the warrior 1953
2 Tam the untamed 1954
3 Treasure of the reef 1955
4 Return to the reef 1956
5 Call of the bush 1959
6 The end of the outlaws 1961
7 The golden wolf 1962
8 Ajax and the drovers 1964
9 Ajax and the haunted mountain 1967

Characters recur between the Brevit and the Ajax series.

Peel, Hazel Mary

ANN AND JIM HENDERSON SERIES:

1 Pilot the hunter 1961
2 Fury son of the wilds 1962
3 Pilot the chaser 1963
4 Easter the show jumper 1965
5 Night storm the flat racer 1966
6 Dido and Rogue 1967
7 Gay Darius 1968

□

1 Jago 1966
2 Untamed 1967

Pemberton, Sir Max

1 The iron pirate 1893
2 Captain Black 1911

Peppe, Rodney

HENRY BOOKS:

1 Henry eats out 1978
2 Henry's aeroplane 1978
3 Henry's exercise 1978
4 Henry's garden 1978
5 Henry's sunbathe 1978
6 Henry's toy cupboard 1978

□

1 The mice who lived in a shoe 1981
2 The Kettleship pirate 1983

Perkins, Al

1 Tubby and the lantern 1972
2 Tubby and the Poo-Bah 1974

See also **Lofting, H.** *and* **Fleming, I.**

Perkins, Janet *and* **John**

1 Haffertee hamster Diamond 1977
2 Haffertee finds a place of his own 1977
3 Haffertee goes exploring 1977
4 Haffertee's first Christmas 1977

Perkins, Lucy Fitch

1 The Dutch twins 1911
2 The cave twins 1922
3 The Irish twins 1922
4 The Scotch twins 1922
5 The Eskimo twins 1922
6 The Chinese twins 1936
7 The Norwegian twins 1936
8 The Spartan twins 1936
9 The Swiss twins 1936
10 The Indian twins 1938
11 The French twins 1939
12 The Belgian twins 1940
13 The pioneer twins 1943
14 The American twins of the Revolution 1943
15 The colonial twins of Virginia 1949
16 The Filipino twins 1949
17 The American twins of 1812 1951
18 The Italian twins 1952
19 The Spanish twins 1952
20 The Japanese twins 1955
21 The Puritan twins 1955
22 The Mexican twins 1955 (continued by D. Rooke)
23 The South African twins
24 The Australian twins

Peterson, Hans

MAGNUS SERIES:

1 Magnus and the squirrel 1960
2 Magnus and the van horse 1961
3 Magnus in the harbour 1962
4 Magnus in danger 1963
5 Magnus and the ship's mascot 1964

□

1 Here comes Peter 1965
2 Peter comes back 1966
3 Peter makes his way 1968
□
1 Lisa settles in 1967
2 Just Lisa 1969
□
1 Sara in summertime 1970
2 Sara and the blue tit 1971
3 Sara and her little brother 1972
□
1 Pelle Janson 1973
2 Pelle in the big city 1975
3 Pelle in trouble 1976
□
1 Erik and the squirrel 1969
2 Erik and the Christmas horse 1969

"Peyo"

1 King Smurf 1978
2 The Smurfette 1978
3 Smurphony in C and flying smurf 1978
4 The Smurfs and the egg and the hundredth smurf 1978
5 The Smurfs and the magic flute 1979
6 The Astro Smurf 1979
7 Romeo and Smurfette 1979
8 The weather Smurfing machine 1979
9 The Smurf's apprentice 1979
10 Smurfic games 1980
11 The Smurfs and the howlbird 1980

3 and 4 include two adventures. 5 was based on the cartoon film of the same title.

Peyton, K. M., *pseud.* **[Kathleen W. Peyton]**

1 Stormcock meets trouble 1961
2 The hard way home 1962
3 Brownsea silver 1964

FLAMBARDS:

1 Flambards 1967
2 The edge of the cloud 1969
3 Flambards in summer 1969
4 Flambards divided 1981

'Flambards' 1978 is an omnibus edition containing 1, 2, 3.

PENNINGTON:

1 Pennington's seventeenth summer 1970
2 The Beethoven medal 1971
3 Pennington's heir 1973
4 Marian's angels 1979

4 is aimed at a much younger age group but Patrick Pennington is a central character.

RUTH HOLLIS:

1 Fly-by-night 1968
2 The team 1975

Ruth Hollis is also a character in the Pennington series and later marries Patrick Pennington.

Phipson, John

THE BARKERS:

1 The family conspiracy 1962
2 Threat to the Barkers 1963

Pienkowski, J., *joint author, see* **Nicoll, Helen** *and* **Pienkowski, Jan**

Piers, Helen

1 Two hungry mice 1966
2 Mouse looks for a house 1967
3 Mouse looks for a friend 1967
4 How did it happen 1967

'The Mouse book' 1972 is an omnibus volume.

□
1 Snail and caterpillar
2 Grasshopper and butterfly

Pilgrim, Jane

BLACKBERRY FARM SERIES:

1 Emily the goat 1949
2 Rusty the sheepdog 1950
3 Postman Joe 1951
4 Mrs Nibble 1949
5 Henry goes visiting 1950
6 Mother Hen and Mary 1951
7 Naughty George 1953
8 Mrs Squirrel and Hazel 1953
9 The birthday picnic 1953
10 Ernest Owl starts a school 1952
11 The adventures of Walter 1952
12 Lucy Mouse keeps a secret 1952
13 Walter Duck and Winifred 1958
14 Mrs Nibble moves house 1957
15 Christmas at Blackberry Farm 1955
16 Sports day at Blackberry Farm 1961
17 Little Martha 1953
18 A bunny in trouble 1960
19 Hide and seek at Blackberry Farm 1959

20 Poor Mr Nibble 1962
21 Snow at Blackberry Farm 1963
22 Sam Sparrow 1965
23 Mr Nibble calls a doctor 1964
24 Saturday at Blackberry Farm 1966
25 Mr Mole takes charge 1967
'Blackberry Farm storybook' 1982 contains 10, 23, 3 and 21.

Plant, Jack
RUSTY MASON
1 Spy trail to danger 1962
2 The league of the purple dagger 1963

Platt, Kin
1 Big Max 1978
2 Big Max in the mystery of the missing moose 1979

Plowman, Stephanie
THE HAMILTON FAMILY:
1 Three lives for the Czar 1969
2 My kingdom for a grave 1970

Plummer, Margaret
1 One rupee and a bundle of rice 1967
2 Rama and the white bullock 1969

Pohl, Frederick *and* **Williamson, J.**
JIM EDEN TRILOGY:
1 Undersea quest 1967
2 Undersea fleet 1968
3 Undersea city 1969

Pope, Ray
1 Strosa light 1966
2 Salvage from Strosa 1967
□
1 The model railway men 1969
2 Telford and the American visitor 1970
3 The model railway-men take over 1971
4 Telford's holiday 1972
5 Telford and the Festiniog railway 1973
6 Telford saves the line 1974
7 Telford goes Dutch 1976
8 Telford tells the truth 1977
9 Model railway-men in America 1978
10 Telford and the prairie battle 1979

Porteous, Richard Sydney
1 Tambai island 1957
2 Tambai treasure 1958
3 The silent isles 1963

Porter, Eleanor Hodgman
1 Pollyanna 1913
2 Pollyanna grows up 1915 (continued by H. L. Smith)
3 Pollyanna of the orange blossoms 1924
4 Pollyanna's jewels 1926
5 Pollyanna's debt of honour 1927
6 Pollyanna's western adventure 1929 (continued by E. Borton)
7 Pollyanna in Hollywood 1931
8 Pollyanna's castle in Mexico 1932
9 Pollyanna's door to happiness 1933
10 Pollyanna's golden horseshoe 1934
11 Pollyanna and the secret mission (continued by M. P. Chalmers)
12 Pollyanna's protegee (continued by V. M. Moffitt)
13 Pollyanna at Six Star Ranch
14 Pollyanna of Magic Valley
□
1 Cross currents 1928
2 The turn of the tide 1928
□
1 Miss Billy 1914
2 Miss Billy – married 1914
3 Miss Billy's decision 1915

Postage, O. *and* **Firmin, P.**
1 Ivor the engine 1962
2 Ivor's outing 1966
'Ivor the Engine storybook' 1982 is an omnibus edition of four stories.
□
1 Bagpuss in the sun 1975
2 Bagpuss on a rainy day 1975
THE SAGA OF NOGGIN THE NOG:
1 King of the Nogs 1968
2 The ice dragon 1969
3 The Omruds 1968
4 The flying machine 1968
5 The island 1969
6 The firecake 1969
7 The flowers 1970
8 The pie 1970
9 The game 1972
10 The monster 1972
11 The backwash 1975
12 The icebergs 1975
□

1 Noggin the King 1965
2 Noggin and the whale 1965
3 Noggin and the dragon 1966
4 Nogbad comes back 1966
5 Noggin and the moon mouse 1967
6 Nogbad and the elephants 1967
7 Noggin and the money 1973
8 Noggin and the storks 1973
Although this series concerns the same characters it has been divided above, since the first series is designed for a rather older age group, the second for young children just starting to read. 'Three tales of Noggin book 1' 1980 is an omnibus of three stories about Noggin. 'Three tales of Noggin book 2' 1980 as above.

Potter, Beatrix
1 The tale of Peter Rabbit 1902
2 The tale of Benjamin Bunny 1904
3 The tale of the flopsy bunnies 1909
4 The tale of Mr Toad 1912
Not strictly sequels but connected. 'The Complete adventures of Peter Rabbit' 1982 includes all four stories.

Potter, M.
THE SINCLAIR FAMILY:
1 The touch and go year 1968
2 The blow and grow year 1970

Preussler, Otfried
1 Robber Hotzenplotz 1970
2 Further adventures of the robber Hotzenplotz 1973
3 The final adventures of the robber Hotzenplotz 1974

Price, Willard
HALL AND ROGER HUNT SERIES:
1 Amazon adventure 1951
2 South sea adventure 1954
3 Underwater adventure 1955
4 Volcano adventure 1956
5 Whale adventure 1960
6 African adventure 1961
7 Elephant adventure 1962
8 Safari adventure 1966
9 Lion adventure 1966
10 Gorilla adventure 1969
11 Diving adventure 1970
12 Cannibal adventure 1972

Provensen, Alice *and* **Martin**
MAPLE HILL FARM
1 The year at Maple Hill Farm
2 A horse and a hound, a goat and a gander

Proysen, Alfred
1 Little old Mrs Pepperpot 1959
2 Mrs Pepperpot again 1960
3 Mrs Pepperpot to the rescue 1963
4 Mrs Pepperpot and the magic wood 1967
5 Mrs Pepperpot's outing 1971
6 Mrs Pepperpot's year 1973
'Mrs Pepperpot's busy day' and 'Mrs Pepperpot's Xmas' are versions of volumes in the series, for younger readers. 'Mrs Pepperpot's first omnibus' 1976 contains 1-3. 'Mrs Pepperpot's second omnibus' 4-6.

Pudney, John
FRED AND I SERIES:
1 Saturday adventure 1950
2 Sunday adventure 1951
3 Monday adventure 1952
4 Tuesday adventure 1953
5 Wednesday adventure 1954
6 Thursday adventure 1955
7 Friday adventure 1956
8 Spring adventure 1961
9 Summer adventure 1962
10 Autumn adventure 1964
11 Winter adventure 1965
□
1 The Hartwarp light railway 1960
2 The Hartwarp dump 1962
3 The Hartwarp circus 1963
4 The Hartwarp balloon 1963
5 The Hartwarp bakehouse 1964
6 The Hartwarp explosion 1965
7 The Hartwarp jets 1967

Pullein-Thompson, *see* **Thompson**

Pye, Virginia
THE PRICE FAMILY:
1 Red-letter holiday 1940
2 Snow bird 1941
3 Primrose Polly 1942
4 Half-term holiday 1943
5 The Prices return 1946

6 The stolen jewels 1958
7 Johanna and the Prices 1951
8 Holiday exchange 1953

Quittenden, R., *pseud.* **[Roland Quiz]**
1 The wonderful adventures of Tom Pippin 1874
2 Tom Pippin's further adventures 1874
3 King Pippin 1874

Rabier, Benjamin
1 Gideon in the Forest 1977
2 Gideon in Africa 1978
3 Gideon 1979
4 Gideon and friends 1979
5 Gideon on the riverbank 1979
6 Gideon's house 1979

Rae, Gwynedd
1 Mostly Mary 1930
2 All Mary 1931
3 Mary Plain in town 1935
4 Mary Plain on holiday 1937
5 Mary Plain in trouble 1940
6 Mary Plain in wartime 1942
7 Mary Plain's big adventure 1944
8 Mary Plain home again 1949
9 Mary Plain to the rescue 1950
10 Mary Plain and the twins 1952
11 Mary Plain goes bob-a-jobbing 1954
12 Mary Plain goes to America 1957
13 Mary Plain, V.I.P. 1961
14 Mary Plain's whodunit 1965

Rae, John
1 The golden crucifix 1974
2 The treasure of Westminster 1975

Ramstedt, Viveka
1 Pickle and Penny 1979
2 Penny and Sue 1980

Ransome, Arthur
1 Swallows and Amazons 1930
2 Swallowdale 1931
3 Peter Duck 1932
4 Winter holiday 1933
5 Coot Club 1934
6 Pigeon post 1936
7 We didn't mean to go to sea 1937
8 Secret water 1939
9 The big six 1940
10 Missee Lee 1941
11 The Picts and the Martyrs 1943
12 Great Northern? 1947
'Ransome revisited' 1975 and 'The travelling Man' 1976 by Elizabeth Mace, are set in a devastated future in which some children find a copy of 'Swallowdale' and set out to find if such a world still exists.

Ray, Mary
1 The Ides of April 1974
2 Sword sleep 1975
3 Beyond the desert gate 1977
4 Shout against the wind 1980
5 Rain from the west 1980

Rayner, Mary
1 Mr and Mrs Pig's evening out 1976
2 Garth Pig and the ice cream lady 1977
3 Mrs Pig's bulk buy 1982

Read, Miss, *pseud.* **[D. J. Saint]**
1 Hobby-horse cottage 1963
2 Hob and the horse bat 1965

Redmond, Phil
1 Grange Hill stories 1979
2 Tucker and Co. 1982
See also **Robert Leeson**

Reeves, James *and* **Ardizzone, Edward**
1 Prefabulous animiles 1974
2 More prefabulous animiles 1975

Reid, Meta Mayne
TIFFANY SERIES:
1 Carrigmore Castle 1954
2 Tiffany and the swallow rhyme 1956
3 The cuckoo at Coolean 1956
4 Strangers in Carrigmore 1958
5 The Tombermillin oracle 1962
THE PEYTON CHILDREN:
1 All because of Dawks 1955
2 Dawks does it again 1956
3 Dawks on Robbers' Mountain 1957
4 Dawks and the duchess 1958
RATHCAPPLE SERIES:
1 Sandy and the hollow book 1961
2 The McNeills at Rathcapple 1962
3 With Angus in the forest 1963

KATE AND LYNN:
1 The tinkers' summer 1965
2 The house at Spaniard's Bay 1967

Reiss, Johanna
1 The upstairs room 1972
2 The journey back 1976

Rey, M. E. *and* **H. A.**
1 Zozo 1942
2 Zozo rides a bike 1954
3 Zozo takes a job 1954
4 Zozo learns the alphabet 1956
5 Zozo gets a medal 1958
6 Zozo flies a kite 1963
7 Zozo goes to the hospital 1967
In the original U.S.A. editions, the main character is 'Curious George'.

Rhodes, J. *and* **Gibbs, S.**
1 Badger's Bend 1964
2 Adventure at Badger's Bend 1965

Richards, Frank, *pseud.* **[Charles Hamilton]**
1 Billy Bunter at Greyfriars school 1947
2 Billy Bunter's balling-out 1948
3 Billy Bunter's banknote 1948
4 Billy Bunter in Brazil 1949
5 Billy Bunter's Christmas party 1949
6 Billy Bunter's benefit 1950
7 Billy Bunter among the cannibals 1950
8 Billy Bunter's postal order 1951
9 Billy Bunter butts in 1951
10 Billy Bunter and the Blue Mauritius 1952
11 Billy Bunter's beanfeast 1952
12 Billy Bunter's brain wave 1953
13 Billy Bunter's first case 1953
14 Billy Bunter the bold 1954
15 Bunter does his best 1954
16 Lord Billy Bunter 1956
17 Backing up Billy Bunter 1955
18 The banishing of Billy Bunter 1956
19 Billy Bunter afloat 1957
20 Billy Bunter the hiker 1958
21 Billy Bunter's bargain 1958
22 Bunter out of bounds 1959
23 Bunter comes for Christmas 1959
24 Billy Bunter's bolt 1957
25 Billy Bunter's double 1955
26 Billy Bunter keeps it dark 1960
27 Bunter the bad lad 1960
28 Bunter the ventriloquist 1961
29 Billy Bunter's treasure hunt 1961
30 Billy Bunter at Butlin's 1961
31 Bunter the caravanner 1962
32 Billy Bunter's bodyguard 1962
33 Just like Bunter 1963
34 Big chief Bunter 1963
35 Bunter the stowaway 1963
36 Thanks to Bunter 1964
37 Bunter the sportsman 1964
38 Bunter's last fling 1965
39 Bunter's holiday cruise 1965
40 Bunter the tough guy of Greyfriars 1965
41 Bunter the racketeer 1965
42 Billy Bunter and the man from South America 1967
43 Billy Bunter and the school rebellion 1967
44 Billy Bunter's big top 1967
45 Billy Bunter and the bank robber 1968
46 Billy Bunter, sportsman 1968
47 Billy Bunter and the crooked captain 1968
48 Billy Bunter's convict 1968
49 Greyfriars rivals 1982
50 Greyfriars actor 1982
51 Bunter's postal order mysteries 1982
Billy Bunter appeared in the Greyfriars school series in the periodical 'Magnet' for over thirty years. Apart from the above, others have appeared in paperback. Frank Richards also writes Bessie Bunter stories (as Hilda Richards).
□
1 Jack the lad
2 Jack at the circus
3 Jack of all trades
TOM MERRY/ST. JIM'S STORIES:
1 Tom Merry's triumph
2 The secret of the study 1949 (as Martin Clifford)
3 The Scapegrace of St. Jim's 1949 (as Martin Clifford)
4 Tom Merry and Co. of St. Jim's 1949 (as Martin Clifford)
5 Rallying round Gussy 1950 (as Martin Clifford)
6 Talbot's secret 1951 (as Martin Clifford)
7 Tom Merry and Co., caravanners (as Frank Richards)
8 Down and out (as Frank Richards)
9 Cardew's catch (as Frank Richards)

10 Through thick and thin (as Frank Richards)
11 The disappearance of Tom Merry (as Frank Richards)
12 Trouble for Tom Merry (as Frank Richards)

MAGNET FACSIMILE REPRINTS:

1 Billy Bunter and the Courtfield cracksman 1970
2 Billy Bunter of Bunter court 1970
3 Billy Bunter and the terror of the form 1970
4 Greyfriars adventures 1972
5 My Lord Bunter 1972
6 Billy Bunter's circus 1974
7 Greyfriars cowboys 1975
8 Bunter's seaside caper 1975
9 Billy Bunter's coronation party 1976
10 Billy Bunter's hair raid 1976
11 Billy Bunter in Brazil 1976
12 Bunter's Christmas party 1976
13 The sheik of Greyfriars 1976
14 Mystery man of Greyfriars 1977
15 Billy Bunter's Easter trip 1977
16 Bounder's rebellion 1977
17 Bunter the hypnotist 1977
18 Billy Bunter's banknotes 1977
19 Billy Bunter, the lion tamer 1977
20 Bunter's funny turn 1977
21 Expelled from Greyfriars 1977
22 Bunter's Christmas carol 1977
23 Bunter's rich relation 1978
24 Greyfriars impersonator 1978
25 Bounder of Greyfriars 1978
26 Big bang at Greyfriars 1978
27 Billionaring with Bunter 1978
28 Billy Bunter of Safari 1978
29 Bunter the bad lad 1979
30 Bully of Greyfriars 1979
31 Greyfriars second eleven 1979
32 Shylock of Greyfriars 1979
33 Billy Bunter's convict 1979
34 Under Bunter's thumb 1980
35 Billy Bunter's prize 1980
36 Greyfriars bounder 1980
37 Greyfriars for grown ups 1980
38 Billy Bunter's blunder 1981
39 Persecution of Billy Bunter 1981
40 Odd fellows of Greyfriars 1981
41 For ever Bunter 1981
42 Greyfriars mysteries 1981
43 Billy Bunter expelled 1982

Richardson, Dorothy

1 The secret Brownies 1979
2 The Brownie ventures 1979
3 The Brownie explorers 1982
4 Brownie rescuers

Richter, H. P.

1 Friedrich 1973
2 I was there 1974
3 The time of the young soldiers 1976

Trilogy of a young German soldier in World War II.

Riddell, James

1 Hit or myth animal lore and disorder 1977
2 Up and down on the farm 1980

Non-fiction.

Riley, A. T.

1 The beginning 1978
2 Way-out East 1978
3 The three wishes 1978
4 A cure for earache 1978

Ringner-Lundgren, E., *see* **Lundgren, E. Ringner**

Rippon, Angela

1 Victoria gives a flying lesson 1981
2 Victoria goes flying 1981
3 Victoria and the prickly hedgehog 1981
4 Victoria's snowflake net 1981

Ritson, K.

TESSA SERIES:

1 Tessa in South Africa
2 Tessa to the rescue 1957
3 Tessa and some ponies 1958
4 The Runnoth dude ranch 1960

Roberts, Doreen

1 Joe at the fair
2 Joe's day at the market

Roberts, Elizabeth

1 Simpey comes to stay 1965
2 Simpey and his grandmother 1967
3 All about Simon and his grandmother 1973

3 is an omnibus of 1 and 2 and some new stories.

Robertson, Jenny
1 Circle of shadows 1980
2 Circle of fire 1980

Robertson, Kate
1 Dilbert wins his wings 1977
2 Dilbert down under 1977
3 Dilbert on Safari 1977
4 Dilbert and the dodo 1977

Robinson, Joan Mary Gale
1 Mary-Mary 1957
2 More Mary-Mary 1958
3 Madam Mary-Mary 1960
'Mary-Mary stories' 1965 is an omnibus volume.
□
1 Teddy Robinson 1953
2 More about Teddy Robinson 1954
3 Teddy Robinson's book 1955
4 Dear Teddy Robinson 1956
5 Teddy Robinson himself 1957
6 Another Teddy Robinson 1960
Reissued in two omnibus editions, 1973 and 1974, with coloured illustrations.

Robinson, Martha
MALTY SERIES:
1 First act 1955
2 Matty in films
3 Matty on television 1959
□
1 The vet's family 1964
2 The vet's son 1966
3 The vet's nieces 1967
4 The vet's problem 1969
5 The vet's holiday 1971

Rockwell, Norman
1 My doctor 1973
2 My nursery school 1976
3 My kitchen 1980

Rodgers, Mary
1 Freaky Friday 1973
2 A billion for Boris 1975
3 Summer switch 1983

Roger Moore and the Crime Fighters
1 The siege (by Malcolm Hulke) 1977
2 1001 shoplifters (by Robin Smythe) 1977
3 Crook ahoy (by Fielden Hughes) 1977
4 The secrets man (by Debden Holt) 1977
5 Anchor trick (by Anthony Wall) 1977
6 Death in denims (by Dulcie Gray) 1977

Rogers, P.
MICHAEL SERIES:
1 Fish and chips 1972
2 The rainy picnic 1973
3 Outing for three 1974

Rogerson, James
KING WILBUR THE THIRD:
1 King Wilbur rebuilds his palace 1976
2 King Wilbur and the bath 1976
3 King Wilbur's birthday present 1976
4 King Wilbur and the bicycle 1976

Romany, *pseud., see* **Evans, G. B.**

Rooke, D.
1 Double Ex 1973
2 A horse of his own 1975
See also **Perkins, L. F.**

Roose-Evans, J., *see* **Evans, J. Roose**

Roso, Gerald
1 PB takes a holiday 1980
2 PB on ice 1982

Ross, Diana
1 Little red engine gets a name 1942
2 Story of the little red engine 1945
3 Little red engine goes to market 1946
4 Little red engine goes to town 1952
5 Little red engine goes travelling 1955
6 Little red engine and the rocket 1956
7 Little red engine goes home 1958
8 Little red engine goes to be mended 1965
9 Little red engine and the Toddlecombe outing 1968
10 Little red engine goes carolling 1971
MISS PUSSY SERIES:
1 The golden hen 1942
2 The wild cherry 1943
3 The enormous apple pie 1951
4 The bran tub 1954
5 The merry-go-round 1963

Ross, Tony
1 Hugo and the man who stole colours 1977

2 Hugo and oddsock 1978
3 Hugo and the ministry of holidays 1980

Rowlands, Avril

GOD'S WONDERFUL RAILWAY:
1 Clear ahead 1980
2 Fire on the line 1981
3 Permanent way 1980

Ruff, Agnes

1 The adventure of Pinkie 1955
2 More adventures of Pinkie 1959

Ruffell, Ann

GRIBBLE THE DRAGON SERIES:
1 Dragon fire 1979
2 Dragon water 1980
3 Dragon earth 1980
4 Dragon air 1981

Rupp, Joanna

1 Rush to the Czech point 1969
2 The Rushes to the rescue 1969

Rush, Caroline

1 Tales of Mr Pengachoosa 1965
2 Further tales of Mr Pengachoosa 1967
'Eight tales of Mr Pengachoosa' 1971 is an omnibus edition.

Rutherford, Douglas

TIM RYDER SERIES: THE CHEQUERED FLAG SERIES:
1 The gunshot grand prix 1972
2 Killer on the track 1973
3 Rally to the death 1974
4 Race against the sun 1976

Ryan, John

1 Captain Pugwash 1957
2 Pugwash aloft 1958
3 Pugwash and the ghost ship 1962
4 Pugwash in the Pacific 1973
5 Pugwash and the sea monster 1976
6 Captain Pugwash and the elephant 1976
7 Pugwash the smuggler 1976
8 The quest of the golden handshake 1983
□
1 Captain Pugwash and the new ship 1976
2 Captain Pugwash and the ruby 1976
3 Captain Pugwash and the treasure chest 1976
4 Pugwash and the buried treasure 1980
5 Pugwash and the fancy-dress party 1982
6 Captain Pugwash and the mutiny 1982
A separate series for younger children.
□
1 Dodo's delight 1977
2 Dodo's homework or the fuddi-duddi-dodo's great mathematical experiment 1978

Ryder, Eileen

1 Tim's new friends
2 Tim's rainy day 1977

Sachs, Marilyn

1 Veronica Ganz 1969
2 Peter and Veronica 1970

Saddler, Allen

KING AND QUEEN SERIES:
1 The archery contest 1982
2 The King gets fit 1982

Saint, D. J., *see* **Read, Miss** *pseud.*

Salkey, Andrew

1 Hurricane 1964
2 Drought 1966
3 Riot 1967
A quartet of stories about the West Indies.

Salten, Felix

1 Bambi 1928
2 Bambi's children 1940

Sampson, Derek

1 Grump and the hairy mammoth 1972
2 Grump strikes back 1973
3 Grump and that mammoth again 1981

Sampson, Fay

1 The watch of Patterick Fell 1978
2 Landfall on Innis Michael 1980

Sandberg, Inger *and* **Lasse**

1 Anna and the magic hat 1966
2 What Anna saw 1966
3 What Anna saved 1966
4 Anna's mother has a birthday 1968
5 When Anna has a cold 1968

6 Little Anna and the tall uncle 1969
7 Where is little Anna's dog 1969
□
1 Kate Kate come and help 1974
2 Kate's bouncy ball 1974
3 Kate's Xmas present 1974
4 Kate's upside down day 1974
These are really continuations of the Anna series, since in the original Swedish, Anne is the main character in all.
□
1 Daniel and the coconut cakes 1973
2 Daniel's mysterious monster 1973
3 Daniel's helping hand 1973
4 Daniel paints a picture 1973
In the original Swedish series the character is called Mathias.
□
1 Johan's year
2 Johan at school 1972
□
1 Little Spook's grubby day 1978
2 Tiny Spook's guessing game 1978
3 Tiny Spook's tumbles 1978
4 Little Spook's baby sister 1978
5 Tiny Spook's tugging game 1978
□
1 Little Spook
2 Little Spook haunts again 1979
3 Little Spook and the lost doll 1979
The second series is in a larger format.

Sandler, Mona
1 Young horse dealers 1957
2 Steep farm stables 1958

Sandwall-Bergstrom, Martha
ANNA SERIES:
1 Anna all alone 1978
2 Anna at Bloom Farm 1978
3 Anna keeps her promise 1978
4 Anna wins through 1979
5 Anna at the manor house 1979
6 Anna solves the mystery 1979

Saunders, M.
1 Beautiful Joe 1894
2 Beautiful Joe's paradise 1903
□
1 True Tilda
2 Tilda Jane's orphans

Saunders, Michael
1 Murphy's mob
2 Murphy and Co. 1983
2 was written by Anthony Masters.

Saville, Malcolm
1 Susan, Bill and the wolf dog 1954
2 Susan, Bill and the ivy-clad oak 1954
3 Susan, Bill and the vanishing boy 1955
4 Susan, Bill and the golden cloak 1955
5 Susan, Bill and the dark stranger 1956
6 Susan, Bill and the Saucy Kate 1956
7 Susan, Bill and the Bright Star circus 1960
8 Susan, Bill and the pirates bold 1961
MICHAEL AND MARY SERIES:
1 Trouble at Townsend 1945
2 The riddle of the painted box 1947
3 The flying fish adventure 1950
4 The secret of the hidden pool 1953
5 Young Johnny Bimbo 1956
6 The fourth key 1957
LONE PINE FIVE CLUB SERIES:
1 Mystery at Witchend 1943
2 Seven white gates 1944
3 Gay dolphin adventure 1945
4 Secret of Grey Walls 1947
5 Lone Pine Five 1949
6 Elusive grasshopper 1951
7 Neglected mountain 1953
8 Saucers over the moon 1955
9 Wings over Witchend 1956
10 Lone Pine London 1957
11 Secret of the gorge 1958
12 Mystery mine 1959
13 Sea witch comes home 1960
14 Not scarlet but gold 1962
15 Treasure at Amory's 1964
16 Man with three fingers 1966
17 Rye Royal 1969
18 Strangers at Witchend 1970
19 Where's my girl 1972
20 Home to Witchend 1979
MARSTON BAINES SERIES:
1 Three towers in Tuscany 1963
2 Purple valley 1964
3 Dark danger 1965
4 White fire 1966
5 Power of three 1968
6 The dagger and the flame 1970
JILLIES SERIES:
1 Redshanks warning 1948

2 Two fair plaits 1948
3 Stranger at Snowfell 1949
4 The sign of the Alpine Rose 1950
5 The luck of Sallowby 1952
6 The Ambermere treasure 1953

BUCKINGHAM SERIES:
1 The master of Maryknoll 1950
2 The Buckinghams at Ravenswyke 1952
3 The long passage 1954
4 A palace for the Buckinghams 1963
5 The secret of Villa Rosa 1971
6 Diamond in the sky 1974

Saward, E., *see* **Doctor Who series**

Sawyer, Ruth
1 Roller skates 1964
2 Lucinda's year of Jubilo 1965

Scarry, Richard
1 Little Richard 1970
2 Little Richard and Prickles 1971

Schmidt, Annie Maria Geertruida
1 Bob and Jilly
2 Bob and Jilly are friends 1978
3 Bob and Jilly in trouble 1980
□
1 Dusty and Smudge spill the paint 1977
2 Dusty and Smudge and the soap suds 1977
3 Dusty and Smudge keep cool 1977
4 Dusty and Smudge and the bride 1977
5 Dusty and Smudge splash the soup 1979
6 Dusty and Smudge and the cake 1979

Schulz, Charles
1 For the love of Peanuts 1967
2 You're a winner, Charlie Brown 1967
3 Fun with Peanuts 1968
4 Good 'Ol Snoopy 1968
5 Here comes Snoopy 1968
6 All this and Snoopy too 1968
7 Good grief Charlie Brown 1969
8 Here's to you Charlie Brown 1969
9 Nobody's perfect Charlie Brown 1969
10 Here comes Charlie Brown 1970
11 We love you Snoopy 1970
12 Peanuts for everybody 1970
13 Charlie Brown and Snoopy 1971
14 It's for you Snoopy 1971
15 What next Charlie Brown 1971
16 You're a pal Snoopy 1972
17 You're not for real Snoopy 1972
18 Your choice Snoopy 1974
19 You've got it made Snoopy 1975
20 You're on your own Snoopy 1976
21 You're something special Snoopy 1977
22 You've come a long way Snoopy 1977
23 You've got to be you Snoopy 1977
24 It's showtime Snoopy 1978
25 It's your turn Snoopy 1978
26 The loves of Snoopy 1978
27 Lucy rules O.K. 1978
28 The misfortunes of Charlie Brown 1978
29 Play ball Snoopy 1978
30 Snoopy and his friends 1978
31 That's life Snoopy 1978
32 It's all yours Snoopy 1979
33 You've got to be kidding Snoopy 1979
34 They're playing your song, Charlie Brown 1979
35 It's raining on your parade, Charlie Brown 1980
36 Let's hear it for dinner, Snoopy 1980
37 The Snoopy festival 1980
38 Think thinner Snoopy 1980
39 Charlie Brown's Christmas 1981
40 It's the great pumpkin Snoopy 1981
41 Jogging is in Snoopy 1981
42 Life is a circus Charlie Brown 1981
43 Love and kisses Snoopy 1981
44 The Snoopy treasury 1981
45 Snoopy's fun and fact books:
  1 Boats 1981
  2 Farms 1981
  3 Houses 1981
  4 Planes 1981
46 Stay with it Snoopy 1981
47 Think about it tomorrow Snoopy 1981
48 Charlie Brown's all stars 1981
49 Blaze the trail Snoopy 1982
50 Happiness is a warm puppy 1982
51 I need all the friends I can get 1982
52 You're a good scout, Snoopy 1982
53 You're our kind of dog Snoopy 1982
54 You're so smart Snoopy 1982
55 Love is walking hand in hand 1982
56 The Peanuts gang 1982
57 The Peanuts gang goes to the circus 1982
58 The Peanuts gang visits a haunted house 1982
59 Snoopy classics 1982
60 Snoopy dog, dog 1982

61 Charlie Brown's great outdoor maze book 1983
62 Where's Snoopy 1983
63 The Peanuts gang on safari 1983
64 This is the best time of day Snoopy 1983
65 Don't give up, Charlie Brown
66 Have it your way Charlie Brown
67 What now Charlie Brown
68 Who was that dog I saw you with
69 You've got a friend Charlie Brown
70 There's no-one like you Snoopy
'Charlie Brown Dictionary' 1979. 'Peanuts Jubilee: my life and art with Charlie Brown and others'. The above is a list of Peanuts publications appearing in various formats.

Scott, Peter G.
1 Into the labrinth
2 Return to the labrinth

Sedwick, M.
1 Adventures of Galldora 1969
2 New adventures of Galldora 1970
3 A rag called Galldora 1971
'The Galldora omnibus' 1973 includes the above and a number of new stories.

Seed, Jenny
1 The voice of the great elephant 1968
2 The price of the bay 1970
3 The broken spear 1972
Stories about the early history of Natal.

Seignobosc, Francoise, *see* **Francoise,** *pseud.* **[Francoise Seignobosc]**

Selden, George
1 The cricket in Times Square 1961
2 Tucker's countryside 1971
3 Harry cat's pet puppy 1978

Selig, Sylvie *and* **Maschler, Fay**
1 T. G. and Moonie move out of town
2 T. G. and Moonie go shopping 1978

Selway, Martina
1 The Grunts go on a picnic 1982
2 The Grunts what a day! 1982

Seredy, Kate
1 The good master 1931
2 The singing tree 1940

Serraillier, Ian
1 They raced for treasure 1946
2 Flight to adventure 1947

Seton, Hilary
MINTY HUMBLE:
1 Beyond the blue hills 1973
2 A lion in the garden 1974

Seuss, Dr.
1 Cat in the hat 1958
2 Cat in the hat comes back 1961

Severn, David
'CRUSOE' SERIES:
1 Rick afire 1942
2 Cabin for Crusoe 1943
3 Wagon for fire 1944
4 Hermit in the hills 1945
5 Forest holiday 1946
WARNER SERIES:
1 Ponies and poachers 1946
2 Cruise of the Maiden Castle 1948
3 Treasure for three 1949
4 Crazy castle 1951
5 Burglars and bandicoots 1952
□
1 Cathedral cat 1965
2 The close cats 1966

Sharmat, Marjorie Weinman
1 Sophie and Gussie 1974
2 The trip and other Sophie and Gussie stories 1978
□
1 Nate the great 1974
2 Nate the great and the lost list 1977
3 Nate the great and the phony clue 1979
□
1 Mooch the Messy 1978
2 Mooch the Messy meets Prudence the neat

Sharp, Margery
MISS BIANCA SERIES:
1 The rescuers 1959
2 Miss Bianca 1962
3 The turret 1964

4 Miss Bianca in the salt mines 1966
5 Miss Bianca in the Orient 1970
6 Miss Bianca in the Antarctic 1971
7 Miss Bianca and the bridesmaid 1972
8 Bernard the brave 1976
9 Bernard into battle 1979

Shaw, Jane
1 Penny foolish 1953
2 Twopence coloured 1954
3 Threepenny bit 1955
4 Fourpenny fair 1956
5 Fivepenny mystery 1958
□
1 Susan pulls the strings
2 Susan's helping hand 1955
3 Susan rushes in 1956
4 Susan interferes 1957
5 Susan at school 1958
6 Susan muddles through 1960
7 Susan's trying term 1961
8 No trouble for Susan 1962
9 Susan's kind heart 1965
10 Where is Susan 1968
11 Job for Susan 1969
□
1 Anything can happen 1964
2 Nothing happened after all 1965
□
1 The Moochers 1950
2 The Moochers abroad 1951

Sheldon, A.
1 Linda Craig: The mystery of Hashoe Canyon 1983
2 Linda Craig: The secret of Rancho del Sol 1983

Shepherd, Jo
1 Huff and Puff
2 Puff in Canada
3 Puff to the rescue

Sherlock, P.
1 The iguana's tail: Crick crack stories from the Caribbean 1977
2 Ears and tails and common sense: More stories from the Caribbean 1979
The author has written collections of stories from other parts of the world.

Sherry, Sylvia
1 Street in the small night market 1966
2 Frog in a coconut shell 1968

Shulman, Milton
1 Preep 1965
2 Preep in Paris 1967
3 Preep and the Queen 1970

Sibley, Kathleen
1 Adam and the football 1974
2 Adam and the F.A. cup 1975
3 Adam and the football mystery 1979

Sidney, Margaret, *pseud.* **[Harriet Mulford Lothrop]**
1 Five little Peppers and how they grew up 1881
2 Five little Peppers midway 1892
3 Five little Peppers grown up 1893
4 Phronsie Pepper 1897
5 The stories of Polly Pepper told
6 The adventures of Joel Pepper

Slater, Jim
1 Grasshopper and the unwise owl 1979
2 Grasshopper and the pickle factory 1980
3 Grasshopper and the poisoned river 1982
□
1 Goldenrod 1978
2 Goldenrod and the kidnappers 1979

Sleigh, Barbara
1 Carbonel 1955
2 The kingdom of Carbonel 1959
3 Carbonel and Calidor 1978

Sloan, Carolyn
1 Mr Cogg and his computer 1970
2 Further inventions of Mr Cogg 1981

Smee, D.
1 Jeremy Smith to the rescue 1958
2 Jeremy Smith investigates 1959
3 Jeremy Smith in trouble 1960
4 Jeremy Smith shows the way 1961

Smith, Mrs Castle, *see* **Brenda,** *pseud.* **[Mrs Castle Smith]**

Smith, Dodie
1 The hundred and one Dalmatians 1956
2 The starlight barking 1967

Smith, Emma
1 Emily 1957
2 Emily's voyage 1966

Smith, Eunice Young
1 The Jennifer wish 1958
2 The Jennifer gift 1959
3 The Jennifer prize 1960
4 Jennifer is eleven 1961
5 Jennifer dances 1962
6 High heels for Jennifer 1965
An Illinois family in the early years of the 20th century.

Smith, H. L.
1 The girls of Friendly Terrace
2 Peggy Raymond's vacation
3 Peggy Raymond's school days
4 The Friendly Terrace quartet
5 Peggy Raymond's way
For the 'Pollyanna' books see under **Porter, E. H.**

Smith, Janet
1 The Wakeley witch 1980
2 The witch, the carpet and boomash 1982

Smith, Jim
1 Nimbus the explorer 1981
2 Nimbus and the crown jewels 1981
□
1 The frog band and the onion-seller 1976
2 The frog band and the Durrington Dormouse 1977
3 The frog band and the owlnapper 1980

Smith, Sam
1 The secret harbour 1975
2 Rover's Regatta day 1977

Smyth, Sir John
ANN SHELTON SERIES:
1 Paradise Island 1958
2 Trouble in Paradise 1959
3 Ann goes hunting 1960

Smythe, Pat
1 Jacqueline rides for a fall 1957
2 Three Jays against the clock 1958
3 Three Jays on holiday 1958
4 Three Jays go to town 1959
5 Three Jays over the border 1960
6 Three Jays go to Rome 1960
7 Three Jays lend a hand 1961
PETER AND CAROL SERIES:
1 A Swiss adventure 1970
2 A Spanish adventure 1971
3 A Cotswold adventure 1973

Smythe, Robin *see* **Roger Moore and the Crime Fighters series**

Soderback, Maruabbe
1 Middles runs away 1969
2 Middles and Tessa 1970

Softly, Barbara
1 Ponder and William 1970
2 Ponder and William at home 1972
3 Ponder and William at the weekend 1974
4 Ponder and William on holiday 1971

Solomon, Joan
1 Berron's tooth 1978
2 Day by the sea 1978
3 Spud comes to play 1978
4 Kate's party 1978
5 Gifts and Almonds 1980
6 Shabnam's day out 1980
7 Present for mum 1981
These feature a group of children, some titles feature the whole group, others concern only one or two.

Sommer-Bodenburg, Angela
1 The little vampire 1982
2 The little vampire moves in 1982

Sommerfelt, Aimée
1 The road to Agra 1961
2 The white bungalow 1963

Southall, Ivan
1 Meet Simon Black 1951
2 Simon Black in peril 1952
3 Simon Black in coastal command 1954
4 Simon Black in China 1955

5 Simon Black and the spacemen 1955
6 Simon Black in the Antarctic 1956
7 Simon Black on Venus 1959
8 Simon Black takes over 1960
9 Simon Black at sea 1961
□
1 King of the sticks
2 Golden goose

Spence, Eleanor
1 The Switherby pilgrims 1967
2 Jamberoo Road

Sperry, Armstrong
CHAD POWELL:
1 The rain forest 1950
2 Thunder country 1953

Sprague, R.
1 A kingdom to win 1953
2 Heroes of the white shield 1955
Historical novels of Olav Trygvason, King of Norway in the 10th century.

Spyri, Johan
1 Heidi's early experiences 1884
2 Heidi's later experiences 1884
Later editions are in one volume, 'Heidi'. Continued by Charles Tritten.
3 Heidi grows up 1938
4 Heidi's children

Steiner, Charlotte
1 Karoleena 1964
2 Karoleena's red coat 1964

Stern, Simon
CAPTAIN KETCHUP SERIES:
1 Neptune's treasure 1972
2 Moon trip 1973
3 Jungle journey 1974
4 Kidnapped

Stevenson, Robert Louis
1 Kidnapped 1886
2 Catriona 1893
'Porto Bello Gold' by A. D. H. Smith is in the form of a prelude to 'Treasure Island' and 'Back to Treasure Island' by H. A. Calahan is a sequel. 'Alan Breck again' by A. D. H. Smith is a sequel to 'Catriona'. 'The return of Long John Silver' by J. Connell and 'Flint's island' by L. Wibberley are also sequels to 'Treasure Island'. 'Adventures of Benn Gunn' by R. F. Delderfield is a foreword telling how Silver lost his leg and the treasure was buried. 'The adventures of Long John Silver' by Denis Judd is also a foreword to 'Treasure Island' and 'Return to Treasure Island' by the same author describes what happened afterwards. 'Silver's revenge' by Robert Leeson also describes happenings after 'Treasure Island'. 'The great book raid' by Christopher Leach also features Long John Silver.

Stiessel, Lena
1 Mick and Muff 1979
2 Mick and Muff in the country 1979
3 Mick and Muff painting 1979
4 Mick and Muff and the little car 1979

Stolz, Mary S.
1 Ready or not 1966
2 The day and the way we met 1956 (USA)

Stone, Bernard
1 Emergency mouse 1978
2 Inspector mouse 1980

Stoneley, Jack
1 The Tuesday dog 1978
2 The return of the Tuesday dogs 1979

Storey, Margaret
TIMOTHY AND MELINDA SERIES:
1 Timothy and the two witches 1966
2 The stone sorcerer 1967
3 The dragon's sister 1967
4 Timothy's travels 1967
5 A quarrel of witches 1970
6 The sleeping witch 1971
7 A war of wizards 1976
8 The double wizard 1979
□
1 The smallest doll 1966
2 The smallest bridesmaid 1966
3 The Mollyday holiday 1971

Storr, Catherine
POLLY AND THE WOLF:
1 Clever Polly 1952
2 Clever Polly and the stupid wolf 1955

3 Polly and the giant's bride 1956
4 Adventures of Polly and the wolf 1957
5 Tales of Polly and the hungry wolf
4 was republished in paperback as 'Polly and the wolf again' 1969.
□
1 Marianne dreams 1958
2 Marianne and Mark 1960
□
1 Lucy 1961
2 Lucy runs away 1962
Omnibus edition 1975.

Stranger, Joyce
1 Paddy Joe 1973
2 Trouble for Paddy Joe 1973
3 Paddy Joe at Deep Hollow Farm 1975
4 Paddy Joe and Tomkin's Folly 1979
TIMOTHY YORK:
1 Vet on call 1981
2 Double trouble 1982
3 Vet riding high 1982

Streatfeild, Noel
1 The Bell family 1954
2 New town 1960
□
1 Thursday's child 1970
2 Far to go 1976
□
1 Meet the Maitlands 1978
2 The Maitlands: all change at Cuckly Place 1979
□
1 Gemma 1968
2 Gemma and sisters 1968
3 Gemma alone 1970
4 Goodbye Gemma 1970

Striker, F.
1 Lone Ranger and the mystery ranch
2 Lone Ranger and the gold robbery
3 Lone Ranger and the outlaw stronghold
4 Lone Ranger and the Bitter Spring feud
5 Lone Ranger and the code of the West
6 Lone Ranger on the Red Button trail

Strode, Warren Chetham
1 Three men and a girl
2 Top of the milk

3 A cat called Tootoo 1966
4 Tootoo's friends at the farm 1967

Strong, J. J.
1 Smith's tail
2 Smith takes a bath

Strutton, B., *see* **Doctor Who series**

Stuart, Sheila
1 Alison's highland holiday 1946
2 More adventures of Alison 1947
3 Alison's Christmas adventure 1948
4 Well done, Alison 1949
5 Alison's Easter adventure 1950
6 Alison's poaching adventure 1951
7 Alison's kidnapping adventure 1952
8 Alison's pony adventure 1953
9 Alison's island adventure 1954
10 Alison's spy adventure 1955
11 Alison and the witch's cave 1956
12 Alison's yacht adventure 1957
13 Alison's riding adventure 1958
14 Alison's cliff adventure 1959
15 Alison's caravan adventure 1960

Styles, Showell
MIDSHIPMAN QUINN SERIES:
1 Midshipman Quinn 1957
2 Quinn of the navy 1958
3 Midshipman Quinn wins through 1961
4 Quinn at Trafalgar 1963
Stories of the Napoleonic war.
SIMON AND MAG SERIES:
1 The shop in the mountains 1960
2 The ladder of snow 1962
3 A necklace of glaciers 1963
4 The pass of morning 1966
5 Journey with a secret 1968
□
1 Indestructible Jones 1967
2 Jones' private navy 1969
□
1 Cubs of the castle 1970
2 Cubs on the job 1972
□
1 The flying ensign
2 Byrd of the 95th 1962
Stories of the Peninsular war.
□
1 Tiger patrol
2 Tiger patrol wins through 1958
□

1 Kidnap castle
2 Traitor's mountain
3 Gideon Hazel

Sudbery, R.

POLLY DEVENISH:

1 The house in the wood 1968
2 Cowls 1969
3 Rich and famous and bad 1970
4 Warts and all 1972
5 Ducks and drakes 1975

Suddaby, Donald

1 New tales of Robin Hood 1950
2 Robin Hood's master stroke 1963

Sustendahl, Pat

STRAWBERRY SHORTCAKE SERIES:

1 Strawberry Shortcake's make and do book 1981
2 Strawberry Shortcake, 1, 2, 3 1981
3 Strawberry Shortcake and the winter that would not end 1982
4 Strawberry Shortcake's sunny day poems 1982

Sutcliff, Rosemary

1 The eagle of the ninth 1954
2 The silver branch 1957

'Three Legions' 1980 is an omnibus volume.

ARTHURIAN BRITAIN:

1 Light beyond the forest: the quest for the Holy Grail 1979
2 The sword and the circle 1981
3 Road to Camlann 1981

Swift, Jonathan

1 Gulliver's travels 1726
2 Mistress Masham's repose (by T. H. White) 1947

2 is the story of a little girl who discovered the descendants of the Lilliputians who had been brought to England.

Swinburne, Doreen

1 Jean tours a hospital 1957
2 Jean becomes a nurse 1958
3 Jean at Jo's hospital 1959
4 Jean S.R.N. 1960
5 Jean's new junior 1964

Swindells, Robert

1 Norah's ark 1979
2 Norah's shark 1979
3 Norah and the whale 1981
4 Norah to the rescue 1981

Sykes, Pamela

1 The Brownies and the fire 1970
2 The Brownies at the zoo 1971
3 The Brownies on the job 1971
4 The Brownies on television 1972
5 The Brownies in hospital 1974
6 The Brownies throw a party 1976

□

1 Come back Lucy 1973
2 Lucy beware 1983

□

1 The flying summer 1969
2 Flight to an island 1970

Symons, Geraldine

PANSY AND ATLANTA SERIES:

1 The workhouse child 1969
2 Miss Rivers and Miss Bridges 1971
3 Mademoiselle 1973

□

1 The rose window 1964
2 The quarantine child 1966

Szudek, Agnes

VICTORIA PLUMB SERIES:

1 Victoria Plumb 1978
2 Victoria and the parrots gang 1979

Tann, Roger

1 Flower power Joe 1980
2 Mac and the caterpillars 1970
3 Maggie in the porridge 1980
4 Six pence for Sam 1980

Tarkington, B.

1 Penrod 1914
2 Penrod and Sam 1916
3 Penrod Jashber 1929

Later published in one volume 'Penrod, his complete story' 1931.

Taro, Oda

PANDA BOOKS:

1 Panda the train driver 1982
2 Panda the doctor 1982
3 Panda the explorer 1982

4 Panda the racing driver 1982
5 Panda the soldier 1982
6 Panda the wizard 1982

Taylor, Jenny *and* **Ingleby, Terry**
1 Messy Malcolm
2 Messy Malcolm's birthday 1978
3 Messy Malcolm's dream 1982

Taylor, Judy
1 Sophie and Jack 1982
2 Sophie and Jack help out 1983

Taylor, Mark
1 Henry the explorer 1967
2 Henry explores the jungle 1969
3 Henry the castaway 1973
4 Henry explores the mountains 1974

Taylor, Mildred D.
1 Roll of thunder, Hear my cry 1977
2 Let the circle be unbroken 1982

Taylor, Reginald
1 Andy and the mascot 1957
2 Andy and the water crossing 1958
3 Andy and the display team 1958
4 Andy and the sharpshooters 1959
5 Andy and the secret papers 1960
6 Andy and the miniature war 1962
7 Andy and the royal review 1963
8 Andy and his last parade 1965

Taylor, Sydney
1 All-of-a-kind family 1961
2 More of all-of-a-kind family 1967

Temple, William Frederick
1 Martin Magnus, Planet Rover 1955
2 Martin Magnus on Mars 1956
3 Martin Magnus on Venus 1957

Thatcher, Doris
1 Henry the helicopter 1960
2 Hovering with Henry 1961
3 Henry the hero 1962
4 Henry in the news 1963
5 Henry's busy winter 1964
6 Henry joins the police 1966
7 Henry and the astronaut 1968
8 Henry and the traction engine 1970
9 Henry in the mountains 1972
10 Henry in Iceland 1973
11 Henry on safari 1975
□
1 Tommy the tugboat 1956
2 Tommy gets a medal 1957
3 Tommy joins the navy 1957
4 Ferryboat Tommy 1959
5 Tommy's new engine 1961
6 Tommy and the onion boat 1965
7 Tommy and the lighthouse 1965
8 Tommy and the oil rig 1967
9 Tommy in the Caribbean 1969
10 Tommy and the Spanish galleon 1969
11 Tommy and the yellow submarine
12 Tommy and the island 1977

Thayer, J.
1 Gus was a friendly ghost 1971
2 What's a ghost going to do 1972
3 Gus and the baby ghost 1973
4 Gus was a Christmas ghost 1973
5 Gus was a Mexican ghost 1975
6 Gus was a gorgeous ghost

Thomas, J. B.
1 The Dragon Green 1974
2 The Prince of the Dragon Green 1975

Thompson, Christine Pullein-
DAVID AND PAT SERIES:
1 The first rosette 1956
2 The second mount 1957
3 Three to ride 1958
4 The lost pony 1958
□
1 The empty field 1961
2 The open gate 1962
□
1 Giles and the elephant
2 Giles and the greyhound
3 Giles and the canal
SANDY AND LAWRENCE:
1 We hunted hounds
2 I carried the horn
3 Goodbye to the hounds
MAJOR HOLBROOKE AND HIS PONY CLUB:
1 Pony club
2 The Radney Riding Club
3 One day event
4 Pony club team
5 Pony club camp 1957

EASTMAN SERIES:

1 The Eastmans in Brittany
2 The Eastmans move house
3 The Eastmans find a boy 1966

PHANTOM HORSE SERIES:

1 Phantom horse comes home
2 Phantom horse goes to Ireland
3 Phantom horse goes to Scotland
4 Phantom horse in danger 1982

□

1 Ponies in the park
2 Ponies in the forest

□

1 Strange riders at Black Pony Inn
2 Mystery at Black Pony Inn
3 Prince at Black Pony Inn
4 Secrets at Black Pony Inn

PONY PATROL:

1 Pony patrol
2 Pony patrol S.O.S.
3 Pony patrol fights back
4 Pony patrol and the mystery horse

Thompson, Diana Pullein-

1 Ponies in the valley
2 A foal for Candy

Thompson, Eric

1 The adventures of Dougal 1971
2 Dougal's Scottish holiday 1971
3 Dougal round the world 1972
4 The misadventures of Dougal 1972
5 Dougal strikes again 1973

Thompson, Josephine Pullein-

1 Fear treks the moor 1979
2 Star riders on the moor 1979
3 Ghost horses on the moor 1980
4 Treasure on the moor 1982

Thompson, Josephine, Diana *and* **Christine, Pullein-**

1 Black Beauty's family 1978
2 Black Beauty's clan 1978

Thompson, Valerie

1 Rough road south
2 Gold on the wind 1977

Thomson, David

DANNY FOX:

1 Danny Fox at the palace 1976
2 Danny Fox meets a stranger 1968

Thomson, Ruth

DETECTIVE PEABODY CASEBOOKS:

1 Peabody's first case 1978
2 Peabody all at sea 1978
3 Detective Peabody—up in the air 1980

Three Investigators series, *see* **Hitchcock, A.**

Thwaite, Ann

JANE AND TOBY SERIES:

1 A seaside holiday for Jane and Toby 1962
2 Toby stays with Jane 1962
3 Toby moves house 1963
4 Jane and Toby start school 1964

Tison, Annette *and* **Taylor, T.**

1 Barbapapa 1970
2 Barbapapa's voyage 1971
3 Barbapapa's ark 1974
4 Barbapapa's school 1976
5 Barbapapa's winter

There is a separate series of paperbacks for younger children.

□

1 Colour and Barbapapa 1978
2 Counting with Barbapapa 1978
3 Shape and Barbapapa 1978

Three books designed for pre-school children to reach them about numbers, shapes and colours.

Titus, Eve

1 Anatole 1957
2 Anatole and the cat 1958
3 Anatole and the robot 1961
4 Anatole over Paris 1962
5 Anatole and the poodle 1966
6 Anatole and the piano 1967
7 Anatole and the thirty thieves 1969
8 Anatole and the toyshop 1970
9 Anatole in Italy 1974

□

1 Basil of Baker Street 1958
2 Basil and the lost colony 1975
3 Basil and the pygmy cats 1977

Todd, Basil Eupham

1 Worzel Gummidge 1936
2 Worzel Gummidge again 1937
3 More about Worzel Gummidge 1938

4 Worzel Gummidge and Saucy Nancy 1947
5 Worzel Gummidge takes a holiday 1949
6 Earthy Mangold and Worzel Gummidge 1954
7 Worzel Gummidge and the railway scarecrows 1955
8 Worzel Gummidge at the circus 1956
9 Worzel Gummidge and the treasure ship 1958
10 Detective Worzel Gummidge 1963

The 'Television adventures of Worzel Gummidge' by Keith Waterhouse and Willis Hall.

□

1 The box in the attic 1970
2 The wand from France 1972

Todd, H. E.

1 Bobby Brewster 1954
2 Bobby Brewster and the winker's club 1949
3 Bobby Brewster's bus conductor 1954
4 Bobby Brewster's shadow 1956
5 Bobby Brewster's bicycle 1957
6 Bobby Brewster's camera 1959
7 Bobby Brewster's wallpaper 1961
8 Bobby Brewster's conker 1963
9 Bobby Brewster detective 1964
10 Bobby Brewster's potato 1964
11 Bobby Brewster's and the ghost 1966
12 Bobby Brewster's kite 1967
13 Bobby Brewster's scarecrow 1968
14 Bobby Brewster's torch 1969
15 Bobby Brewster's balloon race 1970
16 Bobby Brewster's typewriter 1971
17 Bobby Brewster's bee 1972
18 Bobby Brewster's wishbone 1974
19 Bobby Brewster's first film 1974
20 Bobby Brewster's bookmark 1975
21 Bobby Brewster's tea-leaves 1979
22 Bobby Brewster's lamp post 1982

□

1 The sick cow 1974
2 George the fire engine 1976
3 The roundabout horse 1978
4 King of beasts 1979

A series of illustrated picture books, featuring Bobby Brewster.

Tourneur, Dina-Kathelyn

1 Caspar's hair 1976
2 Caspar's ears 1976
3 Caspar's mouth 1976
4 Caspar's feet 1977
5 Caspar's hands 1977
6 Caspar's nose 1977
7 Caspar finds a friend 1980
8 Caspar plants a seed 1980
9 Caspar loses his dog 1980

Townsend, John

1 Rocket ship saboteurs 1960
2 A warning to Earth 1961
3 The secret of Puffin Island 1962

Townsend, John Rowe

1 Gumble's yard 1961
2 Widdershin's Crescent 1965

□

1 Hell's edge 1963
2 The Hallersage sound 1966

Stories set in the imaginary Yorkshire town of Hallersage.

Townson, Hazel

1 The great ice-cream crime 1981
2 The siege of Cobb Street school 1983

Tozer, K.

1 Wanderings of Mumfie 1935
2 Here comes Mumfie 1936
3 Mumfie the admiral 1937
4 Mumfie's magic box 1938
5 Mumfie's Uncle Samuel 1939
6 Mumfie marches on 1942

'Mumfie the elephant' by Marcia Webb, 1977, new adventures for Mumfie.

Tranter, Nigel

KEN AND FIONA SERIES:

1 A Spaniard's isle 1958
2 Border riding 1959
3 Nestor the monster 1960
4 Birds of a feather 1961

DONALD MACDONALD SERIES:

1 Something very fishy
2 Give a dog a bad name 1963
3 Pursuit 1965
4 Fire and high water 1967

□

1 Tinker Tess 1967
2 To the rescue 1968

Travers, Mary
1 Mary Poppins 1934
2 Mary Poppins comes back 1935
3 Mary Poppins opens the door 1944
4 Mary Poppins in the park 1945
5 Mary Poppins in the kitchen 1976
6 Mary Poppins in Cherry Tree Lane 1982

Travis, Falcon
1 Grand howl 1965
2 Tawny talent 1966
3 Tawny trail 1967

Treadgold, Mary
1 The heron ride 1962
2 Return to the heron 1963
□
1 We couldn't leave Dinah 1941
2 The "Polly Harris" 1949
2 was revised and reissued, 1968.
□
1 Elegant Patty 1967
2 Poor Patty 1968

Trease, Geoffrey
1 No boats on Bannermere 1949
2 Under Black Banner 1950
3 Black Banner players 1952
4 Black Banner abroad 1954
5 Gates of Bannerdale 1956
MIKE AND SANDRA:
1 The Maythorn story 1960
2 Change at Maythorn 1962
MARK APPERLEY:
1 Follow my black plume 1963
2 A thousand for Sicily 1964

Treece, Henry
VIKING TRILOGY:
1 Viking dawn 1955
2 The road to Miklagard 1957
3 Viking's sunset 1960
'Last of the Vikings' 1964, 'Swords from the North' 1967 are about Harlad Hardrada, but not sequels.
□
1 Legions of the eagle 1954
2 The eagles have flown 1954
□
1 Ask for King Billy 1955
2 Don't expect any mercy 1958
GORDON STEWART:
1 Killer in dark glasses 1965
2 Bang, you're dead 1966

Trevor, Elleston
THE WOODLANDERS SERIES:
1 Badger's beech 1948
2 The wizard of the wood 1948
3 Badger's moon 1949
4 Mole's castle 1951
5 Sweethallow valley 1951
6 Badger's wood 1958
□
1 The island in the Pines 1948
2 Squirrel's island 1963
□
1 Into the happy glade 1943
2 By a silver stream 1944
3 Green glade 1959

Trimby, Elisa
1 Mr Plum's paradise
2 Mr Plum's oasis 1981

Tring, A. S., *pseud., see* **Meynell, L.**

Tritten, C., *see* **Spyri, J.**

Tucker, Jenni
1 Cubbie's galore
2 Snow Cubby
3 Tree time Cubby
4 Cubby in a muddle

Tully, John
1 Johnny Goodlooks 1977
2 Johnny and the Yank 1978

Tully, Tom
1 Little Ed 1979
2 Little Ed at large 1980
3 Look out – it's Little Ed 1981

Turner, Ethel
1 Seven little Australians 1894
2 The family at Misrule 1895
□
1 The Cub 1915
2 Captain Cub 1917
3 Brigid and the Cub 1919

Turner, Phillip

DARNLEY MILLS SERIES:

1 Colonel Sheperton's clock 1964
2 The Grange at High Force 1964
3 Sea Peril 1966
4 Steam on the line 1968
5 War on the Darnel 1969
6 Devil's nob 1970
7 Powder Quay 1971
8 Dunkirk summer 1973

The locality is the same in all the books, but they are not direct sequels. 4 and 6 are about ancestors of the main characters and are direct sequels.

□

1 Wig-wig and Homer 1969
2 Rookoo and Bree

Uderzo, *joint author, see* **Goscinny, R.** *and* **Uderzo, A.**

Ulyatt, K.

PORTUGEE PHILPS TRILOGY:

1 North against the Sioux 1956
2 The longhorn trail 1967
3 Custer's gold 1971

'Three great westerns' 1973 is an omnibus of the trilogy.

Unnerstad, E.

THE LARSSON FAMILY SERIES:

1 The saucepan journey 1962
2 The Pip-Larssons go sailing 1963
3 The urchin 1964
4 Little O 1965
5 Little O's naughty day

□

1 The spettecake holiday 1958
2 The journey with grandmother 1960
3 Journey to England 1961

Unsworth, Walter

1 Matterhorn man 1964
2 Tiger in the snow 1967
3 Because it is there 1968

Upton, Bertha

1 The adventures of two Dutch dolls and a golliwogg 1895
2 The golliwogg's bicycle club 1896
3 The golliwogg at the sea-side 1896
4 The golliwogg in war 1899
5 The golliwogg's polar adventure 1900
6 The golliwogg's auto go-cart 1901
7 The golliwogg's air-ship 1902
8 The golliwogg's circus 1903
9 The golliwogg in Holland 1904
10 The golliwogg's fox-hunt 1905
11 The golliwogg's desert island 1906
12 The golliwogg's Christmas 1907
13 The golliwogg in the African jungle 1909

Uttley, Alison

LITTLE GREY RABBIT SERIES:

1 The squirrel, the hare and the Little Grey Rabbit 1929
2 How Little Grey Rabbit got back her tail 1930
3 The story of Fuzzypeg the hedgehog 1932
4 Squirrel goes skating 1934
5 Wise Owl's story 1935
6 Little Grey Rabbit's party 1936
7 The knot Squirrel tied 1937
8 Fuzzypeg goes to school 1938
9 Little Grey Rabbit's Christmas 1939
10 Moldy Warp the mole 1940
11 Hare joins the home guard 1942
12 Little Grey Rabbit's washing day 1949
13 Water Rat's picnic 1943
14 Little Grey Rabbit's birthday 1944
15 The speckledy hen 1945
16 Little Grey Rabbit to the rescue (play) 1945
17 Little Grey Rabbit and the weasels 1947
18 Little Grey Rabbit and the wandering hedgehog 1948
19 Little Grey Rabbit makes lace 1950
20 Hare and the Easter eggs 1952
21 Little Grey Rabbit's valentine 1953
22 Little Grey Rabbit goes to sea 1954
23 Little Grey Rabbit's paintbox 1958
24 Little Grey Rabbit and the magic moon 1958
25 Little Grey Rabbit finds a shoe 1960
26 Little Grey Rabbit and the circus 1961
27 Little Grey Rabbit's May Day 1967
28 Little Grey Rabbit goes shopping
29 Little Grey Rabbit's pancake day 1967
30 Little Grey Rabbit's brother
31 Little Grey Rabbit goes to the North Pole 1970
32 Little Grey Rabbit's spring cleaning party 1972

33 Little Grey Rabbit and the snow-baby 1973
34 Hare and the rainbow 1975
'Tales of Little Grey Rabbit' illustrated by Faith Jacques 1980, 'Little Grey Rabbit Storybook' 1977 and 'Little Grey Rabbit's Storybook' 1981, illustrated by Margaret Tempest, are collections of stories.

SAM PIG SERIES:

1 Adventures of Sam Pig 1940
2 Sam Pig goes to market 1941
3 Six tales of Sam Pig 1941
4 Sam Pig and Sally 1942
5 Sam Pig at the circus 1943
6 Sam Pig in trouble 1948
7 Yours ever, Sam Pig 1951
8 Sam Pig and the singing gate 1955
9 Sam Pig goes to the seaside 1960
10 Sam Pig story book 1965

LITTLE BROWN MOUSE SERIES:

1 Snug and Serena meet a queen 1950
2 Snug and Serena pick cowslips 1950
3 Going to the fair 1951
4 Toad's castle 1951
5 Mrs Mouse spring cleans 1952
6 The gypsy hedgehogs 1953
7 Snug and the chimney sweeper 1953
8 The flower show 1955
9 The mouse telegrams 1955
10 Mr Stoat walks in 1957
11 Snug and Serena and the silver spoon 1957
12 Snug and Serena count twelve 1959
13 Snug and Serena go to town 1961

TIM RABBIT SERIES:

1 Adventures of no ordinary rabbit 1937
2 Adventures of Tim Rabbit 1945
3 Tim Rabbit and company 1959
4 Tim Rabbit's dozen 1964

LITTLE RED FOX SERIES:

1 Little Red Fox and the wicked uncle 1954
2 Little Red Fox and Cinderella 1956
3 Little Red Fox and the magic moon 195
4 Little Red Fox and the unicorn 1962
5 Little Red Fox and the big big tree 1968
Collected stories 'Little Red Fox', 'Little Red Fox book 2' and 'More Little Red Fox Stories'.

□

1 Hare and Guy Fawkes 1956
2 Hare goes shopping 1965
3 Fuzzypeg's brother 1971

Vallance, Rosalind

1 Timmy Turnpenny 1937
2 Timmy and Janet 1941
3 Timmy and Roger 1949
4 Timmy in the country 1951
5 Timmy and Bingo 1954
6 Timmy moves house 1956
7 Timmy Turnpenny's secret 1957

TITTYMOUSE SERIES:

1 Tittymouse and Tatty mouse 1946
2 Titty and Tatty by the river 1949
3 Titty and Tatty's house warming 1958

Van Der Meer, Ron *and* Atie

1 My brother Sammy
2 Sammy and Mara
3 Sammy and the cat party 1979
4 Naughty Sammy 1979

□

1 Basil and Boris in London
2 Basil and Boris in North America

Van Leeuwen, Jean

1 Tales of Oliver Pig 1981
2 More tales of Oliver Pig 1981

Van Woerkom, Dorothy O.

1 Abu Ali: Three tales of the Middle East
2 The friends of Abu Ali 1979

Vaughan, Carol

MATILDA SERIES:

1 Missing Matilda 1964
2 Two foals for Matilda 1965
3 The dancing horse 1966
4 Trekker's trail 1967
5 King of the castle 1968

Vendrell, Carme Sole *and* Almirall, Roc

VICTOR AND MARIA SERIES:

1 The coat 1982
2 The cherry tree 1982
3 The climb 1982
4 The bandstand 1982

Vereker, B.

1 Caroline at the film studios 1955
2 Adventure for Caroline 1956

3 Caroline in Scotland 1957
4 Caroline in Wales 1958

Verne, Henry
1 Bob Moran and the Fawcett mystery 1956
2 Bob Moran and the pirates of the air 1957
3 Bob Moran and the sunken galley 1957
4 Bob Moran and the buccaneer's boat 1957
5 Bob Moran and the valley of hell 1958
6 Bob Moran and the fiery claw 1958

Verney, John
THE CALLENDAR FAMILY:
1 Friday's tunnel 1959
2 February's road 1961
3 Ismo 1964
4 Seven sunflower seeds 1968
5 Samson's hoard 1973

Vestly, Anne-Cath
1 Hallo Aurora 1973
2 Aurora and the little blue car 1974
3 Aurora and Socrates 1975
4 Aurora in Holland 1976
□
1 Eight children and a truck 1972
2 Eight children move house 1974
3 Eight children in winter 1976
4 Eight children and Rosie 1977
5 Eight children and the bulldozers 1979

Vincent, Gabrielle
1 Ernest and Celestine 1982
2 Bravo, Ernest and Celestine 1982
3 Smile please, Ernest and Celestine 1982
4 A picnic for Ernest and Celestine 1983
5 Merry Christmas Ernest and Celestine 1983

Viorst, Judith
1 Alexander and the terrible, horrible no good, very bad day 1973
2 Alexander who used to be rich last Sunday 1979

Vipont, Elfrida
THE HAVERARD FAMILY:
1 The lark in the morn 1948
2 The lark on the wing 1950
3 The spring of the year 1957
4 Flowering spring 1960
5 The pavilion 1969
DOWBIGGINS SERIES:
1 Family at Dowbiggins 1955
2 More about Dowbiggins 1958
3 Changes at Dowbiggins 1960
This series was retitled and reissued as follows: (1) Terror by night, (2) Beggars and receivers, (3) A win for Henry Conyers.

Virin, A.
1 Elsa tidies her house 1974
2 Elsa's bears 1974
3 Elsa in the night 1974
4 Elsa's bears need the doctor
5 Elsa's bears in the playground 1978
6 Elsa's bears learn to paint 1978

Voegeli, Max
ADVENTURES OF ALI:
1 The wonderful lamp 1959
2 Prince of Hindustan 1960

Voilier
TV ADVENTURES OF THE FAMOUS FIVE:
1 Famous Five and the missing cheetah 1981
2 Famous Five and the mystery of the emeralds 1981
3 Famous Five and the stately home gang 1981
4 Famous Five go on T.V. 1981
5 Famous Five and the golden galleon 1982
6 Famous Five and the black mask 1982
7 Famous Five and the blue bear mystery 1983
8 Famous Five in fancy dress 1983

Waber, Bernard
1 Lyle, Lyle, crocodile 1966
2 Lovable Lyle 1970
3 Lyle and the birthday party 1967
4 Welcome Lyle 1969
5 Lyle finds his mother 1976

Wahl, Jan
MELVIN SPITZNAGLE:
1 The furious flycycle 1970
2 S.O.S. Bobomoble 1975
□

1 The Muffletump storybook 1975
2 The Muffletumps' Christmas party 1977
3 The Muffletumps' Halloween scare 1977
□
1 Pleasant Fieldmouse 1969
2 Pleasant Fieldmouse storybook 1978
3 Pleasant Fieldmouse's Halloween party 1976
4 Pleasant Fieldmouse's valentine trick 1977

Wahstedt, V.
1 A present for Granny 1971
2 Ann and Susie pick berries 1972
3 Ann and Susie keep shop 1973
4 Granny's secret attic 1974
5 Goodbye Ann and Susie 1977

Wakefield, S. A.
1 Bottlesnikes and Gumbles 1975
2 Gumbles on guard 1976
3 Gumbles in summer 1980

Walker, A. P.
1 Told by the Sandman
2 The Sandman's tales
3 The Sandman's hour
4 The Sandman's twilight stories
5 The Sandman's Christmas stories
6 The Sandman's rainy day stories
7 The Sandman's stories of Drusilla Doll

Walker, Frank
1 Vipers and Co.
2 Pop go the Vipers 1978

Walker, Victoria
1 The winter of enchantment
2 The house called Hadlows

Wall, Anthony, *see* **Roger Moore and the Crime Fighters series**

Wallace, Ivy Lilian
1 The story of Pookie 1953
2 Pookie at the seaside 1956
3 Pookie's big day 1958
4 Pookie and the swallows 1963
5 Pookie in wonderland 1963
6 Pookie and tne gypsies 1964
7 Pookie puts the world right 1966
8 Pookie in search of a home
9 Pookie believes in Santa Claus 1965
10 Pookie and his shop 1967
□
1 The young Warrenders 1961
2 Thanks to Peculiar 1962
3 Strangers at Warrenders Halt 1963
4 The snake ring mystery 1965

Walsh, Jill Paton
1 Goldengrove 1972
2 Unleaving 1976
□
1 Toomaker 1973
2 The walls of Athens 1977
3 Persian gold 1978

Walters, Hugh
CHRIS GODFREY SERIES:
1 Blast off at Woomera 1957
2 The domes of Pico 1958
3 Operation Columbus 1960
4 Moon base one 1961
5 Expedition Venus 1962
6 Destination Mars 1963
7 Mission to Mercury 1965
8 Journey to Jupiter 1965
9 Spaceship to Saturn 1966
10 The Mohole mystery 1967
11 Nearly Neptune 1969
12 First contact 1971
13 Passage to Pluto 1973
14 Murder on Mars
15 The caves of Drach 1977
16 The last disaster 1978
17 The blue aura 1979
18 The dark triangle 1981
□
1 Boy astronaut
2 First family on the moon 1979

Warner, P. M.
1 A friend for Frances 1956
2 If it hadn't been for Frances 1957

Waterhouse, Keith *and* **Hall, Willis**
WORZEL GUMMIDGE:
1 Worzel Gummidge at the fair
2 Worzel Gummidge goes to the seaside
3 Television adventures of Worzel Gummidge
4 More television adventures of Worzel Gummidge

5 Worzel's birthday
6 Worzel and Aunt Sally: the new television adventures 1983
'Worzel Gummidge cookbook' 1979 by Valerie Hall. Based on characters created by B. E. Todd but stories taken from the television series.

Watanabe, Shigeo
1 How do I put it on? 1979
2 Hallo! How are you? 1980
3 How do I eat? 1980
4 I can do it! 1982
5 I'm the king of the castle 1982
6 I can build a house 1983

Waterman, Jill
1 Harry's colours 1979
2 Harry's spots 1979
3 Harry's stripes 1980
4 Harry's numbers 1983

Waters, Frank, *ed.*
1 Reading with mother
2 More reading with mother 1976
3 Playtime reading with mother 1979
Collections of stories for using with young children.

Watkins-Pritchford, D. J., *see* **B. B.** *pseud.*

Watts, Marjorie-Ann
1 Crocodile medicine 1977
2 Crocodile plaster 1978

Wayne, Jennifer
THE WINCHESTER FAMILY SERIES:
1 The day the ceiling fell down 1961
2 The night the rain came in 1963
3 Merry by name 1964
4 The ghost next door 1965
5 Someone in the attic 1967
6 Something in the barn 1971
□
1 Sprout 1970
2 Sprout window cleaner 1971
3 Sprout and the dog sitter 1972
4 Sprout and the helicopter 1974
5 Sprout and the conjuror 1976

Webb, K.
1 Nat's braces 1982
2 Nat's hat 1982

Weber, L.
1 Meet the Malones 1944
2 Beany Malone 1948
3 Beany has a secret life 1955
4 Happy birthday dear Beany 1957

Webster, Jean
1 Daddy long-legs 1912
2 Dear enemy 1915
□
1 When Patty went to college 1903
2 Just Patty 1911

Webster, Joanne
1 Nobody's horse 1975
2 Horse on a hilltop 1976
3 Horses is like people 1979

Weir, Rosemary
1 The secret journey 1957
2 The secret of Cobbett's farm 1957
□
1 No. 10 Green Street 1958
2 Great days in Green Street 1960
□
1 Albert the dragon 1961
2 Further adventures of Albert the dragon 1964
3 Albert the dragon and the centaur 1968
4 Albert and the dragonettes 1977
5 Albert's world tour 1978

Welch, Ronald
CAREY FAMILY SERIES:
1 Knight crusader 1954
2 The hawk 1967 (Elizabeth I)
3 For the King 1961 (English Civil War)
4 Captain of the dragoons 1956 (Marlborough)
5 Mohawk valley 1958 (18th century Canadian frontier war)
6 Escape from France 1960 (French Revolution)
7 Captain of foot 1959 (Peninsular war)
8 Ensign Carey 1976 (Indian mutiny)
9 Nicholas Carey 1963 (Crimean war)
Historical novels of a single family. Order above is chronological rather than publication order.

Wells, B.

1 Five-yard Fuller 1964
2 Five-yard Fuller and the unlikely knights 1967

Wells, H.

1 Cherry Ames student nurse
2 Cherry Ames senior nurse
3 Cherry Ames flight nurse
4 Cherry Ames cruise nurse
5 Cherry Ames chief nurse
6 Cherry Ames boarding school nurse
7 Cherry Ames visiting nurse
8 Cherry Ames private duty nurse
9 Cherry Ames department store nurse
10 Cherry Ames mountaineer nurse
11 Cherry Ames camp nurse
12 Cherry Ames island nurse
13 Cherry Ames army nurse
14 Cherry Ames at Hilton Hospital
15 Cherry Ames clinic nurse
16 Cherry Ames at Spencer
17 Cherry Ames night supervisor
18 Cherry Ames rest home nurse
19 Cherry Ames country doctor's nurse
20 Cherry Ames dude ranch nurse
Nos 15-20 were written by J. Tatham.
□
1 Silver wings for Vicki
2 Vicki finds the answer
3 Hidden valley mystery
4 Secret of Magnolia Manor

Wells, Rosemary

1 Max's first word 1980
2 Max's new suit 1980
3 Max's ride 1980
4 Max's toys: A counting book 1980

Wensell, Ulises

JACKSON FAMILY SERIES:
1 Mum and Dad 1977
2 Jenny and Steve 1977
3 Smudge 1977
4 Grandma and Grandpa Jackson 1978
5 Granny and Grandad Parker 1978
6 Everyday life 1978
7 Our friends 1978
8 Our home 1978
9 Uncle George and Aunt Mary 1978

Westall, Robert

1 The machine gunners 1975
2 Ghost after ghost (comp. by Aidan Chambers) 1982
3 Fathom five 1982
4 The haunting of Chas McGill 1983
2 is a collection of short stories by various authors. Westall has written one story featuring 'Chas McGill', a central character in 'The Machine gunners'.

Westwood, A. M.

1 The riddle of Kittiwake Rock 1959
2 Trouble at Kittiwake Rock 1960

Whitaker, David, *see* **Doctor Who series**

White, C. A.

1 The ballet school mystery
2 Dancer's daughter

White, C. M.

JOANNA BRADLEY SERIES:
1 Cadet nurse at St. Mark's 1961
2 Junior nurse at St. Mark's 1962
3 Nurse at St. Mark's 1963
4 Staff nurse at St. Mark's 1966
5 Suspect at St. Mark's 1972

White, Paul

1 Jungle doctor 1950
2 Jungle doctor on safari 1950
3 Jungle doctor operates 1950
4 Jungle doctor meets a lion 1950
5 Jungle doctor attacks witchcraft 1951
6 Jungle doctor's enemies 1951
7 Jungle doctor to the rescue 1951
8 Jungle doctor's casebook 1952
9 Jungle doctor and the whirlwind 1952
10 Eyes on the Jungle doctor 1953
11 Jungle doctor looks for trouble 1953
12 Doctor of Tanganyika 1952
13 Jungle doctor hunts big game 1956
14 Jungle doctor's monkey tales 1957
15 Jungle doctor on the hop 1957
16 Jungle doctor's crooked dealings 1958
17 Jungle doctor stings a scorpion 1959
18 Jungle doctor's tug of war 1960
19 Jungle doctor spots a leopard 1961
20 Jungle doctor pulls a leg 1962

White, P. *and* **Britten, D.**
1 The mystery miler 1960
2 Ructions at Ranford 1961
3 Ranford goes fishing 1962

Whitlock, Judith
1 The green bunyip 1962
2 Bunyip at the seaside 1962
3 Bunyip and the Brolga bird 1963
4 Bunyip and the bushfire 1964
5 Bunyip and the tiger cats 1965

Whittle, Tyler
1 Spades and feathers 1955
2 The runners of Orford 1956
3 Castle lizard 1957

Wibberley, Leonard
1 John Treegate's musket 1959
2 Peter Treegate's war 1960
3 Treegate's raiders 1962
Stories of the American Revolution.
□
1 Encounter near Venus 1968
2 Journey to Untor 1971
See also **Stevenson, R. L.**

Wiggin, Kate Douglas
1 Rebecca of Sunnybrook Farm 1903
2 New chronicles of Rebecca 1905
3 More about Rebecca 1970
2 and 3 are the same book.

Wild, Robin *and* **Jocelyn**
1 The Bears' A.B.C. 1977
2 The Bears' counting book 1978
□
1 Spots Dogs and the Alley cats 1979
2 Spots Dogs and the kidnappers 1981

Wilder, Laura I.
LAURA INGALLS SERIES:
1 Little House in the big woods 1956
2 Little House on the prairie 1957
3 On the banks of Plum Creek 1958
4 By the shores of Silver Lake 1961
5 The long winter 1962
6 Little town on the prairie 1963
7 These happy golden years 1964
8 The first four years 1973
'Farmer boy' 1965 is the story of the boyhood of Almanzo Wilder, the future husband of Laura. 'Young Pioneers' 1979 is by Rose Wilder Lane (daughter of Laura) based on the story of her own family. 'West from home' 1976 is a collection of letters from Laura to Almanzo. 'The Little House omnibus' 1978 contains 1-3.

Willard, Barbara
1 Snail and the Pennithornes 1957
2 Snail and the Pennithornes next time 1958
3 Snail and the Pennithornes and the Princes 1960
JILL AND LIMPET:
1 A dog and a half 1964
2 Surprise island 1966
□
1 The Dippers and Jo 1960
2 The Dippers and the high-flying kite 1963
MANTLEMASS SERIES:
1 The lark and the laurel 1970
2 A spring of broom 1971
3 A cold wind blowing 1972
4 The iron lily 1973
5 Harrow and harvest 1974
6 The Miller's boy 1976
7 The eldest son 1977
8 A flight of swans 1980
9 The keys of Mantlemass 1981
THE TOWER FAMILY:
1 The family Tower 1968
2 The toppling Towers 1969

Williams, D.
1 Wendy wins a pony 1961
2 Wendy wins her spurs 1962
3 Wendy at Wembley 1963
4 Wendy goes abroad 1964

Williams, Ferelith Eccles
1 One old Oxford Ox
2 The Oxford Ox's alphabet 1977
3 The Oxford Ox's calendar 1980

Williams, Gladys
1 Semolina Silkpaws comes to Catstown 1962
2 Fireworks for Semolina Silkpaws 1964
3 Semolina Silkpaws' motor car 1968
4 Semolina Silkpaws takes a holiday abroad 1972

Williams, Jay *and* **Abrashkin, R.**

1 Danny Dunn and the homework machine 1958
2 Danny Dunn and the anti-gravity paint 1959
3 Danny Dunn time traveller 1965
4 Danny Dunn and the small flying machine 1965
5 Danny Dunn and the ocean floor 1966
6 Danny Dunn and the automatic house 1967
7 Danny Dunn on a desert island 1968
8 Danny Dunn and the voice from space 1969
9 Danny Dunn and the fossil cave 1971
10 Danny Dunn and the swamp monster 1972
11 Danny Dunn and the universal glue 1972
12 Danny Dunn and the heat ray 1973
13 Danny Dunn invisible boy 1974
14 Danny Dunn and the weather machine 1975
15 Danny Dunn, scientific detective 1976

Williams, Ursula Moray

1 The Binklebys at home 1951
2 The Binklebys on the farm 1953
□
1 The three toymakers 1945
2 Malkin's mountain 1948
3 The toymaker's daughter 1968

Williamson, J., *joint author, see* **Pohl, F.** *and* **Williamson, J.**

Willson, R. B.

SARAH AND ALISTAIR SERIES:
1 Leopards on the Loire 1962
2 A seraph in a box 1963
3 Pineapple palace 1964

Wilson, A. C.

1 Norman Bones detective 1949
2 Norman and Henry Bones 1952
3 Norman and Henry Bones investigate 1953
4 Norman and Henry Bones solve the problem 1957
5 Norman and Henry follow the trail 1959

Wilson, Bob

1 Stanley Bagshaw and the fourteen foot wheel 1981
2 Stanley Bagshaw and the twenty two ton whale 1982

Wilson, David H.

1 Elephants don't sit on cars
2 Getting rich with Jeremy James 1979
3 Beside the sea with Jeremy James 1980

Wilson, Eric

1 Murder on the Canadian 1976
2 Vancouver nightmare 1978
3 Terror in Winnipeg 1979

Wilson, Forrest

1 Super Gran
2 Super Gran rules O.K.
3 Super Gran is magic 1983

Wingate, John

1 Submarine Sinclair 1960
2 Jimmy-the-one 1960
3 Sinclair in command 1961
4 Nuclear captain 1962
5 Sub-zero 1963
6 Full fathom five 1967
7 In the blood 1973

Wolde, Gunilla

1 Emma quite contrary 1974
2 Emma's baby brother 1974
3 Emma and the measles 1975
4 Emma goes to the dentist 1975
5 Different Peter and Emma 1975
6 Emma and the vacuum cleaner 1975
7 Emma's first day at nursery school 1976
8 Emma enjoys nursery school 1976
9 Emma and the doctor 1977
10 Emma's workshop 1977
□
1 Thomas builds a house 1971
2 Thomas goes out 1971
3 Thomas has a bath 1971
4 Thomas tidies his room 1971
5 Thomas and Sarah dress up 1972
6 Thomas goes to the doctor 1972
7 Thomas bakes a cake 1974
8 Thomas is little 1974
9 Thomas and his cat 1975
10 Thomas is different 1975

Wolff, Margaret

BOOKS FOR ME SERIES:

1 Me 1978
2 All about me 1978
3 My bathtime 1978
4 My day 1978
5 My new baby 1979
6 Me in puddles 1979
7 What I can do 1979
8 Me outside 1979
9 My bedroom 1980
10 Me shopping 1980
11 My toys 1980
12 My pussycat 1980
13 My dinner 1983
14 My teddy 1983
15 My truck 1983
16 What I wear 1983

Wood, Joyce

1 Grandmother Lucy and her hats 1969
2 Grandmother Lucy goes for a picnic 1970
3 Grandmother Lucy in her garden 1972
4 Grandmother Lucy's birthday 1973

Wood, K.

1 Gulls
2 A period of violence 1977

Wood, Leslie *and* **Burden, Roy**

1 Count with us from the big red bus 1978
2 Shapes we see from the big red bus 1978
3 Patterns we see from the big red bus 1978
4 Compare with us from the big red bus 1978
5 Measure with us from the big red bus 1978
6 Sets we see from the big red bus 1978
Maths books using theme of people on the bus and things seen on the way.

Wood, Lorna

HAG DOWSABLE AND THE LINDLEY CHILDREN:

1 People in the garden 1954
2 Rescue by broomstick 1954
3 The Hag calls for help 1957
4 Seven-league ballet shoes 1959
5 Hags on holiday 1960
6 Hag in the castle 1962
7 Hags by starlight 1970

□

1 The dogs of Pangers 1970
2 Panger's pup 1972

Woodberry, Joan

1 Rafferty takes to fishing 1959
2 Floodtide for Rafferty 1960
3 Rafferty rides a winner 1961
4 Rafferty makes a landfall 1962

Woodfield, H.

1 Mister Penny 1958
2 Mister Penny's racehorse 1959

Woolsey, S. C., *see* **Coolidge, S.,** *pseud.* **[S. C. Wolsey]**

Worthington, Phoebe *and* **Selby**

1 Teddy bear coalman 1977
2 Teddy bear baker 1979
3 Teddy bear postman 1981
4 Teddy bear gardener 1983

Wright, Kit

1 Arthur's granny 1978
2 Arthur's sister 1978
3 Arthur's father 1978
4 Arthur's uncle 1978

Wright, Kit *and* **Chapman, Gillian**

1 Professor Potts meets the animals in Africa 1981
2 Professor Potts meets the animals in North America 1981
3 Professor Potts meets the animals in Asia 1981

Wrightson, Patricia

THE COLLINS CHILDREN:

1 The crooked snake 1955
2 The Bunyip Hole 1958
3 Nargun and the stars 1973
4 The ice is coming 1977

Wyatt, W.

1 Mr Saucy Squirrel 1972
2 Further exploits of Mr Saucy Squirrel 1977

Yates, Elizabeth

1 Patterns on the wall 1943
2 Hue and cry 1953
New England family life in the early 19th century.
□
1 Mountain born 1951
2 A place for Peter 1952

Yeoman, John

1 The bear's winter house 1969
2 The bear's water picnic 1970

York, Andrew

JONATHAN ANDERS SERIES:
1 The doom fishermen 1969
2 Manhunt for a general 1970
3 Appointment in Kiltone 1972

Young, Mike

1 Superted in the Creepy Castle 1980
2 Superted in space 1980
3 Superted and the lost ponies 1980
4 Superted and the helicopter pirates 1980
5 Superted and the green planet 1980
6 Superted at the bottom of the sea 1981
7 Superted meets Zappy and Zoppy 1981
8 Superted and the giant kites 1983
9 Superted and the Inca treasure 1983
10 Superted and the pearl fishers 1983
11 Superted and the stolen rocket ship 1983

Zabel, Jennifer

1 Miss Priscilla scares them stiff
2 Miss Priscilla's secret 1978
3 Miss Priscilla strikes again 1979

Zindel, Paul

1 The pigman 1969
2 The pigman's legacy 1980

Zinkin, Taya

1 Rishi 1960
2 Rishi returns 1961

Zion, Gene

1 No roses for Harry 1961
2 Harry the dirty dog 1960
3 Harry and the lady next door 1962
4 Harry by the sea 1966

AWARD WINNERS

Boston Globe/Horn Book Awards

The Awards go to the authors of non-fiction and fiction books and illustrators of books for children.

1967 Fiction – HAUGAARD, ERIK CHRISTIAN
The little fishes
Illustration – SPIER, PETER
London Bridge is falling down

1968 Fiction – LAWSON, JOHN
The spring rider
Illustration – LENT, BLAIR
Tikki Tikki Tembo

1969 Fiction – LE GUIN, URSULA
The Wizard of Earthsea
Illustration – GOODALL, JOHN S.
The adventures of Paddy Pork

1970 Fiction – TOWNSEND, JOHN ROWE
The intruder
Illustration – KEATS, EZRA JACK
Hi, Cat!

1971 Fiction – CAMERON, ELEANOR
A room made of windows
Illustration – BURNINGHAM, JOHN
Mr Gumpy's outing

1972 Fiction – SUTCLIFF, ROSEMARY
Tristan and Iseult
Illustration – MIZUMURA, KARNE
If I built a village

1973 Fiction – COOPER, SUSAN
The dark is rising
Illustration – PYLE, HOWARD
King Stork

1974 Fiction – HAMILTON, VIRGINIA
M. C. Higgins, the Great
Illustration – FEELINGS, MURIEL
Jambo means hello: Swahili alphabet book

1975 Fiction – DEGENS, T.
Transport 7-41-R
Illustration – ANNO, MITSMASA
Anno's alphabet

1976 Fiction – WALSH, JILL PATON
Unleaving
Non-Fiction – TAMARIN, ALFRED and GLUBOK, SHIRLEY
Voyaging to Cathay
Illustration – CHARLIP, REMY and JOYNER, JERRY
Thirteen

1977 Fiction – YEP, LAWRENCE
Child of the owl
Non-Fiction – DICKINSON, PETER
Chance, luck and destiny
Illustration – TRIPP, WALLACE
Grandfa' Grig had a pig and other rhymes without a reason from Mother Goose

1978 Fiction – RASKIN, ELLEN
The Westing game
Non-Fiction – KOEHN, ILSE
Mischling: A second degree: my childhood in Nazi Germany
Illustration – ANNO, MITSMASA
Anno's journey

1979 Fiction – FLEISCHMAN, SID
Humbug mountain
Non-Fiction – KHERDIAN, DAVID
The road from home: the story of the Armenian Girl
Illustration – BRIGGS, RAYMOND
The snowman

1980 Fiction – DAVIES, ANDREW
Conrad's war
Non-Fiction – SALVADORI, MARIO
Building: the fight against gravity
Illustration – ALLSBURG, CHRIS VAN
The garden of Abdul Gasazi

1981 Fiction – HALL, LYNN
The leaving
Non-Fiction – LASKY, KATHRYN
The Weaver's gift
Illustration – SENDAK, MAURICE
Outside over there

1982 Fiction – PARK, RUTH
Playing Beatie Bow
Non-Fiction – SIEGAL, ARANKA
Upon the head of the goat: a childhood in Hungary 1939-1944
Illustration – WILLARD, NANCY
A visit to William Blake's Inn

Caldecott Medal

Given to the most distinguished American picture book for children published in the preceding year.

1938 LATHROP, DOROTHY P.
Animals of the Bible, a picture book

1939 HANDFORTH, THOMAS
Mei Li

1940 D'AULAIRE, INGRI *and* EDGAR
Abraham Lincoln

1941 Lawson, Robert
They were strong and good
1942 McCloskey, Robert
Make way for ducklings
1943 Burton, Virginia Lee
The little house
1944 Slobodkin, Louis
Many moons by James Thurber
1945 Jones, Elizabeth Orton
Prayer for a child by Rachel Field
1946 Petersham, Maud *and* Miska
The rooster crows
1947 Weigsgard, Leonard
The little island by Golden MacDonald
1948 Duvoisin, Roger
White snow, bright snow by Alwin Tresselt
1949 Hader, Berta *and* Elmer
The big snow
1950 Politi, Leo
Song of the swallows
1951 Milhous, Katherine
The egg tree
1952 Mordinoff, Nicolas
Finders Keepers by Will Lipkind *and* Nicolas Mordinoff
1953 Ward, Lynd
The biggest bear
1954 Bemelmans, Ludwig
Madeline's rescue
1955 Brown, Marcia
Cinderella, or the glass slipper
1956 Rojankovsky, Feodor
Frog went a-courtin' by John Langstaff
1957 Simont, Marc
A tree is nice by Janice May Udry
1958 McCloskey, Robert
Time of wonder
1959 Cooney, Barbara
Chanticleer and the fox
1960 Ets, Marie Hall
Nine days to Christmas
1961 Sidjakov, Nicolas
Baboushka and the three kings
1962 Brown, Marcia
Once a mouse
1963 Keats, Ezra Jack
The snowy day
1964 Sendak, Maurice
Where the wild things are
1965 Montresor, Beni
May I bring a friend? by Beatrice S. de Regniers
1966 Hogrogian, Nonny
Always room for one more
1967 Ness, Evaline
Sam, Bangs and Moonshine
1968 Emberley, Ed
Drummer Hoff
1969 Shulevitz, Uri
The fool of the world and the flying ship by Arthur Ransome
1970 Steig, William
Sylvester and the magic pebble
1971 Haley, Gail E.
A story-a story: an African tale
1972 Hogrogian, Nonny
One fine day
1973 Lent, Blair
The funny little woman by Arlene Mosel
1974 Zemach, Margot
Duffy and the devil retold by Harvey Zemach
1975 McDermott, Gerald
Arrow to the sun: a Pueblo Indian tale
1976 Dillon, Leo *and* Diane
Why mosquitoes buzz in people's ears: a West African tale retold Verna Aardema
1977 Dillon, Leo *and* Diane
Ashanti to Zulu: African traditions retold by Margaret Musgrove
1978 Spier, Peter
Noah's Ark
1979 Goble, Paul
The girl who loved wild horses
1980 Cooney, Barbara
Ox cart man
1981 Lobel, Arnold
Fables
1982 Allsburg, Chris Van
Jumanjii

Carnegie Medal

Awarded annually for an outstanding book for children written in English and receiving its first publication in the United Kingdom during the preceding year.

1936 Ransome, Arthur
Pigeon Post
1937 Garnett, Eve
The family from One End Street
1938 Streatfeild, Noel
The circus is coming

1939 Doorly, Eleanor
The Radium Woman
1940 Barne, Kitty
Visitors from London
1941 Treadgold, Mary
We couldn't leave Dinah
1942 'BB' (D. J. Watkins-Pitchford)
The little grey men
1943 Award withheld
1944 Linklater, Eric
The wind on the moon
1945 Award withheld
1946 Goudge, Elizabeth
The little white horse
1947 de la Mare, Walter
Collected stories for children
1948 Armstrong, Richard
Sea change
1949 Allen, Agnes
The story of your home
1950 Vipont, Elfrida Foulds
The lark on the wing
1951 Harnett, Cynthia
The wool-pack
1952 Norton, Mary
The borrowers
1953 Osmond, Edward
A valley grows up
1954 'Welch, Ronald' (Felton, Ronald Oliver)
Knight Crusaders
1955 Farjeon, Eleanor
The little bookroom
1956 Lewis, C. S.
The last battle
1957 Mayne, William
A grass rope
1958 Pearce, Philippa A.
Tom's midnight garden
1959 Sutcliff, Rosemary
The lantern bearers
1960 Cornwall, Ian
The making of man
1961 Boston, Lucy, M.
A stranger at Green Knowe
1962 Clarke, Pauline
The twelve and the genii
1963 Burton, Hester
Time of trial
1964 Porter, Sheena
Nordy Bank
1965 Turner, Philip
The Grange at High Force
1966 Award withheld
1967 Garner, Alan
The owl service
1968 Harris, Rosemary
The man in the cloud
1969 Peyton, Kathleen
The edge of the cloud
1970 Garfield, Leon *and* Blishen, Edward
The god beneath the sea
1971 Southall, Ivan
Josh
1972 Adams, Richard
Watership Down
1973 Lively, Penelope
The ghost of Thomas Kempe
1974 Hunter, Mollie
The stronghold
1975 Westall, Robert
The machine gunners
1976 Mark, Jan
Thunder and lightnings
1977 Kemp, Gene
The turbulent term of Tyke Tyler
1978 Rees, David
The Exeter blitz
1979 Dickinson, Peter
Tulku
1980 Dickinson, Peter
City of gold
1981 Westhall, Robert
The scarecrows

Eleanor Farjeon Award

1966 onwards, awarded for 'distinguished services to children's books'.

1975 Lewis, Naomi
1976 Oldmeadow, Joyce *and* Court
1977 Moss, Elaine
1978 Kennerley, Peter
1979 Whitby, Joy
1980 Butler, Dorothy
1981 Marshall, Margaret
Jensen, Virginia
1982 Chambers, Aidan *and* Nancy

Federation of Children's Book Groups—Children's Book Award

1980 Blake, Quentin
Mr. Magnolia
1981 Garfield, Leon
Fair's fair

Greenaway Medal

Awarded to the artist who, in the opinion of The Library Association, has produced the most distinguished work in the illustration of children's books first published in the United Kingdom during the preceding year.

1955 Award withheld
1956 ARDIZZONE, EDWARD
Tim all alone
1957 DRUMMOND, V. H.
Mrs. Easter and the storks
1958 Award withheld
1959 STOBBS, WILLIAM
Kashtanka and A bundle of ballads
1960 ROSE, GERALD
Old Winkle and the seagulls
1961 MAITLAND, ANTONY
Mrs. Cockle's cat
1962 WILDSMITH, BRIAN
A B C
1963 BURNINGHAM, JOHN
Borka: the adventures of a goose with no feathers
1964 HODGES, C. WALTER
Shakespeare's theatre
1965 AMBRUS, VICTOR G.
The three poor tailors
1966 BRIGGS, RAYMOND
Mother Goose treasury
1967 KEEPING, CHARLES
Charley, Charlotte and the golden canary
1968 BAYNES, PAULINE
Dictionary of chivalry
1969 OXENBURY, HELEN
The Quangle Wangle's hat
1970 BURNINGHAM, JOHN
Mr. Gumpy's outing
1971 PIEWKOWSKI, JAN
The kingdom under the sea
1972 TURSKA, KRYSTYNA
The woodcutter's duck
1973 BRIGGS, RAYMOND
Father Christmas
1974 HUTCHINS, PAT
The wind blew
1975 AMBRUS, VICTOR
Horses in battle and *Mishka*
1976 HALEY, GAIL
The Post Office cat
1977 HUGHES, SHIRLEY
Helpers
1978 AHLBERG, JANET
Each peach, pear, plum
1979 PIEWKOWSKI, JAN
Haunted house
1980 BLAKE, QUENTIN
Mr. Magnolia
1981 KEEPING, CHARLES
The Highwayman
1982 FOREMAN, MICHAEL
Thunderfoot and long neck
Sleeping Beauty (Angela Carter)

The Guardian Award

Given for an outstanding work for children by a citizen of the Commonwealth published during the preceding year.

1975 COWLEY, WINIFRED
Gran at Coalgate
1976 BAWDEN, NINA
The peppermint pig
1977 DICKINSON, PETER
The Blue Hawk
1978 JONES, DIANA WYNNE
A charmed life
1979 DAVIES, ANDREW
Conrad's war
1980 SCHLEE, ANNE
The vandal
1981 CARTER, PETER
The sentinels
1982 GARDAM, JANE
The hollow land
1982 MAGORIAN, MICHELLE
Goodnight Mister Tom
1983 DESAI, ANITA
The village by the sea

Hans Christian Andersen International Medal

Awarded to a living author and a living artist for an outstanding body of work that has made an important contribution to children's literature.

1956 ELEANOR FARJEON United Kingdom
1958 ASTRID LINDGREN Sweden
1960 ERICH KASTNER Germany
1962 MEINDERT DEJONG USA
1964 RENE GUILLOT France
1966 ALOIS CARIGIET (author) Switzerland
TOVE JANSSON (illustrator) Finland
1968 JAMES KRUSS (author) Germany
JOSE MARIA SANCHEZ SILVA (author) Spain
JIRI TRNKA (illustrator) Czechoslovakia

1970 Gianni Rodari (author) Italy
Maurice Sendak (illustrator) USA
1972 Scott O'Dell (author) USA
Ib Spang Olsen (illustrator) Denmark
1974 Maria Gripe (author) Sweden
Farshid Misghali (illustrator) Iran
1976 Bødker, Cecil (author) Denmark
Mawrina, Tatjana (illustrator) USSR
1978 Fox, Paula (author) USA
Sven, Otto S. (illustrator) Denmark
1980 Riha, Bohumil (author) Czechoslovakia
Akaba, Suekichi (illustrator) Japan
1982 Nunes, Lygia Bojunga (author) Brazil
Rychlicki, Zbigniew (illustrator) Poland

John Newbery Medal

Awarded annually for the most distinguished contribution to children's literature during the preceding year.

1922 Van Loon, Hendrik Willem
The story of mankind
1923 Lofting, Hugh
The voyages of Doctor Dolittle
1924 Hawes, Charles Boardman
The dark frigate
1925 Finger, Charles J.
Tales from silver lands
1926 Chrisman, Arthur Bowie
Shen of the sea
1927 James, Will
Smoky, the cowhorse
1928 Mukerji, Dham Gopal
Gay-neck, the story of a pigeon
1929 Kelly, Eric P.
The trumpeter of Krakow
1930 Field, Rachel
Hitty, her first hundred years
1931 Coatsworth, Elizabeth
The cat who went to Heaven
1932 Armer, Laura Adams
Waterless mountain
1933 Lewis, Elizabeth Foreman
Young Fu of the Upper Yangtze
1934 Meigs, Cornelia
Invincible Louisa
1935 Shannon, Monica
Dobry
1936 Brink, Carol Ryrie
Caddie Woodlawn
1937 Sawyer, Ruth
Roller skates
1938 Seredy, Kate
The white stag
1939 Enright, Elizabeth
Thimble summer
1940 Daugherty, James
Daniel Boone
1941 Sperry, Armstrong
Call it courage (published in GB as *The boy who was afraid*)
1942 Edmonds, Walter D.
The matchlock gun
1943 Gray, Elizabeth Janet
Adam of the road
1944 Forbes, Esther
Johnny Tremain: A novel for old and young
1945 Lawson, Robert
Rabbit Hill
1946 Lenski, Lois
Strawberry girl
1947 Bailey, Carolyn Sherwin
Miss Hickory
1948 Pene du Bois, William
The twenty one balloons
1949 Henry, Marguerite
King of the wind
1950 D'Angeli, Marguerite
The door in the wall
1951 Yates, Elizabeth
Amos Fortune, free man
1952 Estes, Eleanor
Ginger Pye
1953 Clark, Ann Nolan
Secret of the Andes
1954 Krumgold, Joseph
. . . and now Miguel
1955 DeJong, Meindert
The wheel on the school
1956 Latham, Jean Lee
Carry on, Mr. Bowditch
1957 Sorensen, Virginia
Miracles of Maple Hill
1958 Keith, Harold
Rifles for Watie
1959 Speare, Elizabeth George
The witch of Blackbird Pond
1960 Krumgold, Joseph
Onion John
1961 O'Dell, Scott
Island of the Blue Dolphins
1962 Speare, Elizabeth George
The bronze bow
1963 L'Engle, Madeleine
A wrinkle in time
1964 Neville, Emily
It's like this, cat
1965 Wojciechowska, Maia
Shadow of a bull

1966 DE TREVINO, ELIZABETH B.
I, Juan de Pareja
1967 HUNT, IRENE
Up a road slowly
1968 KONIGSBURG, ELAINE L.
From the mixed-up files of Mrs. Basil E. Frankweiler
1969 ALEXANDER, LLOYD
The high king
1970 ARMSTRONG, WILLIAM H.
Sounder
1971 BYARS, BETSY
Summer of the swans
1972 O'BRIEN, ROBERT C.
Mrs. Frisby and the rab of NIMH
1973 GEORGE, JEAN CRAIGHEAD
Julie of the wolves
1974 FOX, PAULA
The slave dancer
1975 HAMILTON, VIRGINIA
M. C. Higgins the great
1976 COOPER, SUSAN
The grey king
1977 TAYLOR, MILDRED D.
Roll of thunder, hear my cry
1978 PATERSON, KATHERINE
Bridge to Terabithia
1979 RASKIN, ELLEN
The westing game
1980 BLOS, JOAN W.
A gathering of days: a New England girl's journal
1981 PATERSON, KATHERINE
Jacob, have I loved
1982 WILLARD, NANCY
A visit to William Blake's Inn

Kurt Mashler Award

For a work of imagination in the children's field in which text and illustration are of excellence and so presented that each enhances yet balances the other.

1982 CARTER, ANGELA (author)
FOREMAN, MICHAEL (artist)
The Sleeping Beauty and other favourite fairy tales

The Mother Goose Award

Awarded to the most exciting newcomer to have illustrated a picture book in the preceding year.

1979 CARTLIDGE, MICHELLE
Pippin and Pop
1980 CARTWRIGHT, REG
Mr. Potter's pigeon
1981 WIJNGARRD, JUAN
Greenfinger House by Rosemary Harris
1982 ORMEROD, JAN
Sunshine

The Other Award

The award is made annually for 'non-biased books of literary merit'.

1975 MACGIBBON, JEAN
Hal
PRICE, SUSAN
Twopence a tub
EDWARDS, DOROTHY
Joe and Timothy together
1976 ASHLEY, BERNARD
The trouble with Donovan Croft
FITZHUGH, LOUISE
Nobody's family is going to change
HUGHES, SHIRLEY
Helpers
1977 KEMP, GENE
The turbulent term of Tyke Tyler
DHONDY, FARRUKH
East End at your feet
Kestrel's People Working series
The work of Frederick Gríce
1978 SUTCLIFF, ROSEMARY
Song for a dark Queen
DAVIDSON, BASIL
Discovering Africa's past
WATERSON, MARY
Gypsy family
NAUGHTON, BILL
The goalkeeper's revenge and other stories
1979 DHONDY, FARRUKH
Come to Mecca and other stories
CATE, DICK
Old dog, new tricks
MILLS, ROGER
A comprehensive education, 1965-75
WAGSTAFF, SUE
Two Victorian families
1980 REES, DAVID
The green bough of liberty
LULING, VIRGINIA
Aborigines
BULL, ANGELA
The machine breakers: the story of the Luddites
AHLBERG, ALLAN
Mrs. Plug the plumber

1981 Edwards, Dorothy
A strong and willing girl
Althea
What is a union?
Thomson, Ruth
Have you started yet?: all about periods and how to cope with yours
Heaslip, Peter *and* Griffiths, Anne
The terraced house books (set D)
1982 Purkis, Sallie
Into the past 1-4
Ajegbo, Keith
Black lives, white worlds
Hemmings, Susan
Girls are powerful
Shyer, Marlene Fanta
Welcome home, Jellybean
Briggs, Raymond
When the wind blows

Signal Poetry Award

1979 onwards. Awarded for an outstanding poetry book for children.

1979 Hughes, Ted
Moon-bells and other poems
1980 No award

Times Educational Supplement Information Books Award

Senior 1972 onwards, junior 1974 onwards. For outstandingly good information books originating in any Commonwealth country.

1975 Junior (up to age of 9)
Whitlock, Ralph
Spiders
Senior (between 10 and 16)
Flanagan, Geraldine L. *and* Morris, Sean
Window into a nest
1976 Junior
Allen, Eleanor
Wash and brush up
Senior
Encyclopaedia of Africa
1977 Junior
Mabey, Richard
Street flowers
Senior
Mitchell, James
Man and machines
1978 Junior
Barber, Richard
Tournaments
Senior
Gray, Dulcie
Butterflies on my mind
1979 Junior
Bernard, George
The common frog
Senior
Cousins, Jane
Make it happy: what sex is all about
1980 Junior
Updegraf, Robert *and* Imelda
Earthquakes and volcanoes
Senior
Hurd, Michael (ed)
Oxford Junior Companion to Music
1981 Junior
No award
Senior
Steel, Richard
Skulls

Whitbread Children's Book Award

For an outstanding book for children of sever and over.

1976 Lively, Penelope
A stitch in time
1977 McDonald, Sheilagh
No end to yesterday
1978 Pearce, Philippa
The battle of Bubble and Squeak
1979 Dickinson, Peter
Tulku
1980 Garfield, Leon
John Diamond
1981 Gardam, Jane
The hollow land
1982 Corbett, William
Song of Pentecost

'Young Observer'/Rank Organisation Fiction Prize

For the best fiction work for teenage readers written by a citizen of the Commonwealth, Republic of Ireland, Pakistan or Republic of South Africa.

1981 Strachan, Ian
Moses Beech
1982 Mark, Jan
Aquarius
Melwood, Mary
The watcher bee